MY LANGUAGE JOURNAL

THIS JOURNAL BELONGS TO

_____

COPYRIGHT © 2019 PolyglotPanda.com
All rights reserved

Gina Mullaney

When I started learning my first language, I read this:

> "If you talk to a man in a language he understands, that goes to his head.
> If you talk to him in his language, that goes to his heart."
>
> – Nelson Mandela

Now, almost 7 years later, I'm a polyglot. I speak 5 languages and I'm currently learning my 6th one.

Here's to every single dreamer willing to speak to people's hearts

While traditional textbooks certainly help with studying a new language, a lot of learners find that unconventional methods can do a lot to stimulate language mastery and memory. One great, hands-on supplement to textbooks and language-learning apps is journaling.

Language journals and notebooks are a fun way to personalize and document your experience, and they also make the perfect travel companion. Not to mention, writing things down improves our ability to remember them. The main idea is that you guide your own learning by recording vocabulary and other language concepts you run into. It's a way to make language learning more personal, and a lot more engaging.

That's something I always try to teach my students. In order to learn a language, you must make it your own. You have to be passionate about it, love it and enjoy every second you spend with it. Otherwise, you won't ever get to speak the language.

That's is why, after so many years coaching people on language learning and helping people reach their goals with Spanish, Italian and English (*these are a some of the languages I teach*), I have created this Language Learning Journal, so my students (*and everyone else*) can take advantage of the power of journaling to boost their language skills.

When you create an organized system for your activities, you can better manage your time and energy. As I usually say in my masterclasses and courses, if you're trying to master a foreign language, organizing the process is the first thing you should do. That's why all courses contain modules and lessons. It's structure. As a learner, however, you have to create your own structure. That's where the language journal comes in.

Let's take a look at your new pal in the language adventure:

[6]

1 — 2

Do you know what a foreign accent is? It's a sign of bravery
AMY CHUA
— 3 —

Today's work

Active Passive

☑ _____ ☐ ☐
☑ _____ ☐ ☐
☑ _____ 4 _____ ☐ ☐
☑ _____ ☐ ☐

Things I have memorized   5

• •
• •
• •

things I still can't remember

6

Season

Episode

Minute

7

⁉ Have you forced yourself today to speak the language with someone?   YES   NO

NOTES

_____ 8 _____
_____
_____

Every day you will be required to fulfill two pages. There's a total of 17 sections per day to be fulfilled. As you will see, you will be covering every single aspect of your language learning. In these sections you will find nothing less than 7 years of experience teaching languages and the approval of thousands of students that have reached their goals with me.

1.- A box for the current date is shown by the 📅 icon

2.- The STREAK METER is a numerical representation of your dedication and perseverance. It is represented by the 🎖 icon. Each day in a row that you work on the target language, you add +1. If you skip one day (*and it was not planned to be skipped*), the streak meter comes back to 0. Try to not break the streak and get to the biggest number possible.

3.- A thoughtful learning-related quote to motivate you.

4.- A space to write down the exact exercises you have done today. It can be anything like *"writing a 120-words text about my family"* or *"Pages 44-45 of the textbook"*. On the right side you can check if it was an active or a passive exercise.

5.- An Up/Down box to fulfill with three things you were able to remember for the first time and three things you are still unable to remember no matter as hard as you try. In this section, you want to celebrate those words you always forgot but you didn't today and write down once more those your brain still can't retain.

6.- Using Netflix, HBO, Amazon…? Use this box to write down which episode you are on. If you need to write down the title of the series, use the screen space.

7.- Simple but effective question. Answering this question will force you to speak the language with someone in order to check "YES".

8.- Any thought about today's work.

9.- When studying, it is normal to leave incomprehensible things for later or store questions in our head that we need to solve later on. Make sure to write down everything you have to look up the next day so you don't forget.

10.- Review the vocabulary you have learned today. You can use each hexagon for a word (*10 words*) or use a row of them to write the original words in the first hexagon and the translation in the second one (*5 words*).

11.- Obviously your main goal is to learn a certain language. But, as you probably know if you have taken classes with me, it is indispensable to break down your main goal into several specific goals. In this section, you can write tiny goals like "*Finish chapter 4 of the Spanish book*" or "*listen Podcast n°28*" and their deadline ("*Thursday*", "*January*" "*11/7*"...)

12.- Learning a new language is a wonderful experience filled with silly little things that fill us with happiness. The first time you say "*Estoy caliente*" in Spanish ("*I'm horny*") when trying to say "*I'm hot*". The first time you have a phone conversation in the language and you don't understand anything at all. The first time a friend of yours gets surprised when he discovers you speak another language. All these silly incredible things must be written down in here.

13 & 14.- Motivational questions. If you need to add more information apart from "*yes*" or "*no*", use the notes section (*8*).

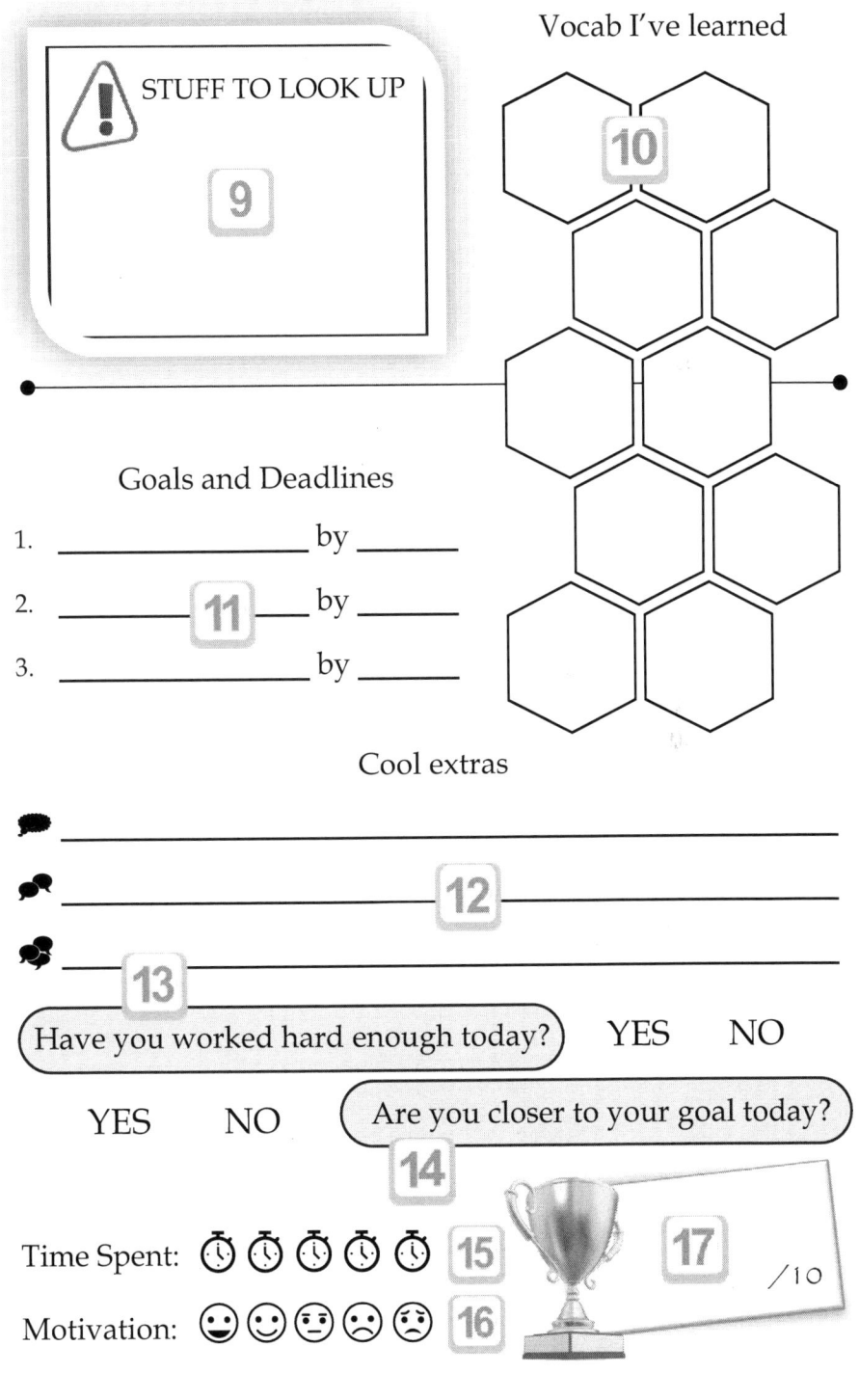

15.- Mark the amount of time you spend working on the language. Each ⏱ can take any value (*E.g.: 5min, 15min…*)

16.- Mark your level of motivation today. It is normal to not feel super motivated every single day. These icons will help you check how productive you are depending on your motivation level. But remember that having low motivation is no excuse for not working on your goal (*you don't want to break your streak, do you?* 👀)

17.- Total score out of 10. This is a personal subjective score you give to yourself based on everything you have written down on the journal. You have to consider the work you've done, streak number, goals, extras, time spent, motivation and the answers to the questions. Here's my personal trick: set a reward for when you achieve a high score (*8, 9 or 10*) and let you enjoy it. I have changed my rewards over the years (*because my personal situation has changed as well*) but some of them were playing Age of Empires (*my fav PC game*), 10 minutes in the hot tub or watching FRIENDS (*my fav sitcom*).

When you start journaling your new adventure there are several things you are going to notice. They are the same things my students tell me when they start a new journal:

- Don't know what kind of stuff goes into the notes section: The more you use this journal the more you will feel like there are things that don't fit in any other section. Each person has their own methods and likings to learn a language. What about if you like to learn languages with an app like Duolingo or Memrise? The notes section can be very helpful for that.
- The answer to section 7 is always "*NO*": The answer to that question will always be "*NO*" because it feels horrible when you expose yourself talking in another

language to anyone else. You feel insecure, silly and embarrassed. You are outside your comfort zone. But, you like it or not, doing it is essential in order to master a language. So you have to do it. And how do we force ourselves to speak in other languages? By making ourselves feel bad for answering "*NO*" every single time we fill this journal.

- The "*Cool Extras*" section is always empty: This is the exact same case as before. You have to push yourself outside the comfort zone where those cool extras happen. Don't worry if that section feels empty at the beginning. You will start filling it up with time.
- It is impossible to get a streak higher than 10: Journaling is not a miracle. You need perseverance and dedication to work on your goal every single day and write down the process in a journal. With time you will acquire the necessary habits to learn languages on your own. If you need extra help, you will find many productivity tricks on my website www.polyglotpanda.com.

Now, just to make sure you understood how to get the most of this journal, on the next page I'll give you a realistic example of how it must be filled. If you still have doubts about how to use this journal or you need any kind of help or coaching, feel free to email me to info@polyglotpanda.com.

📅 17/5/2020   48 🏆

Do you know what a foreign accent is? It's a sign of bravery
AMY CHUA

Today's work

                                                      Active   Passive

- [x] Podcast "A mi aire" ep. 367 + Excercises 3-4   ☒   ☒
- [x] Write 30-word text with political vocab   ☒   ☐
- [x] Review vocab Group 3 + Group 4   ☒   ☐
- [x] 20 min "FRIENDS" w/ subtitles   ☐   ☒

Things I have memorized

- A pesar de (despite)
- Para mi
- Langosta (lobster)
- Ser/Estar!!!
- Pronounce "chaleco"
- hot ≠ horny

things I still can't remember

Season 2 Episode 12 Minute 7:49

⁉️ Have you forced yourself today to speak the language with someone?   ~~YES~~ *!!!*   NO

NOTES

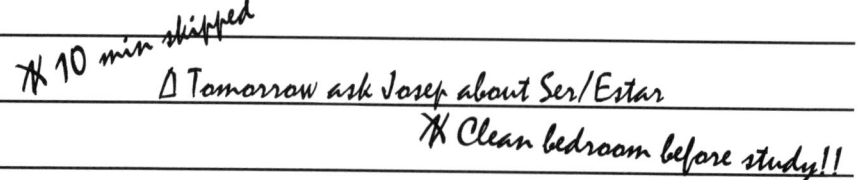

✱ 10 min ~~skipped~~
△ Tomorrow ask Josep about Ser/Estar
✱ Clean bedroom before study!!

⚠ STUFF TO LOOK UP
* SER VS ESTAR
* Pronunciation "chaleco"
* How to ask for a cigarette

Vocab I've learned

- Como — How
- Rata — Rat
- cuadro — picture
- Rey — King
- Pavo — Turkey

Goals and Deadlines

1. Finish chapter 4 by 1/6
2. Email to Josep by Friday
3. Prep. DELE B1 by 7/7

Cool extras

💬 Embarrassed does not mean EMBARAZADO (pregnant)!!!
💬 Waiter didn't understand my Spanish HAHAHA!!
💬 Heard an ad in Spanish about hemorrhoids and understood it

Have you worked hard enough today?   ⊙YES⊙   NO

YES   NO   Are you closer to your goal today?

Time Spent: ⏱ ⏱ ⏱ ⏱̶ ⏱
Motivation: ❌ 😊 😐 🙁 😟

8,5 /10

Are you ready for your new adventure?

Remember that if you have any doubt or need any help, you can contact me at **info@polyglotpanda.com**. Also, if you have a complaint about this journal or you find any mistake, feel free to contact me and I will try to amend the error as soon as possible.

It's time to work hard
to improve your life!

[18]

Do you know what a foreign accent is? It's a sign of bravery
AMY CHUA

Today's work

Active Passive

☑ _____ ☐ ☐
☑ _____ ☐ ☐
☑ _____ ☐ ☐
☑ _____ ☐ ☐

Things I have memorized

things I still can't remember

Season

Episode

Minute

⁉ Have you forced yourself today to speak the language with someone?   YES   NO

NOTES

_____
_____
_____

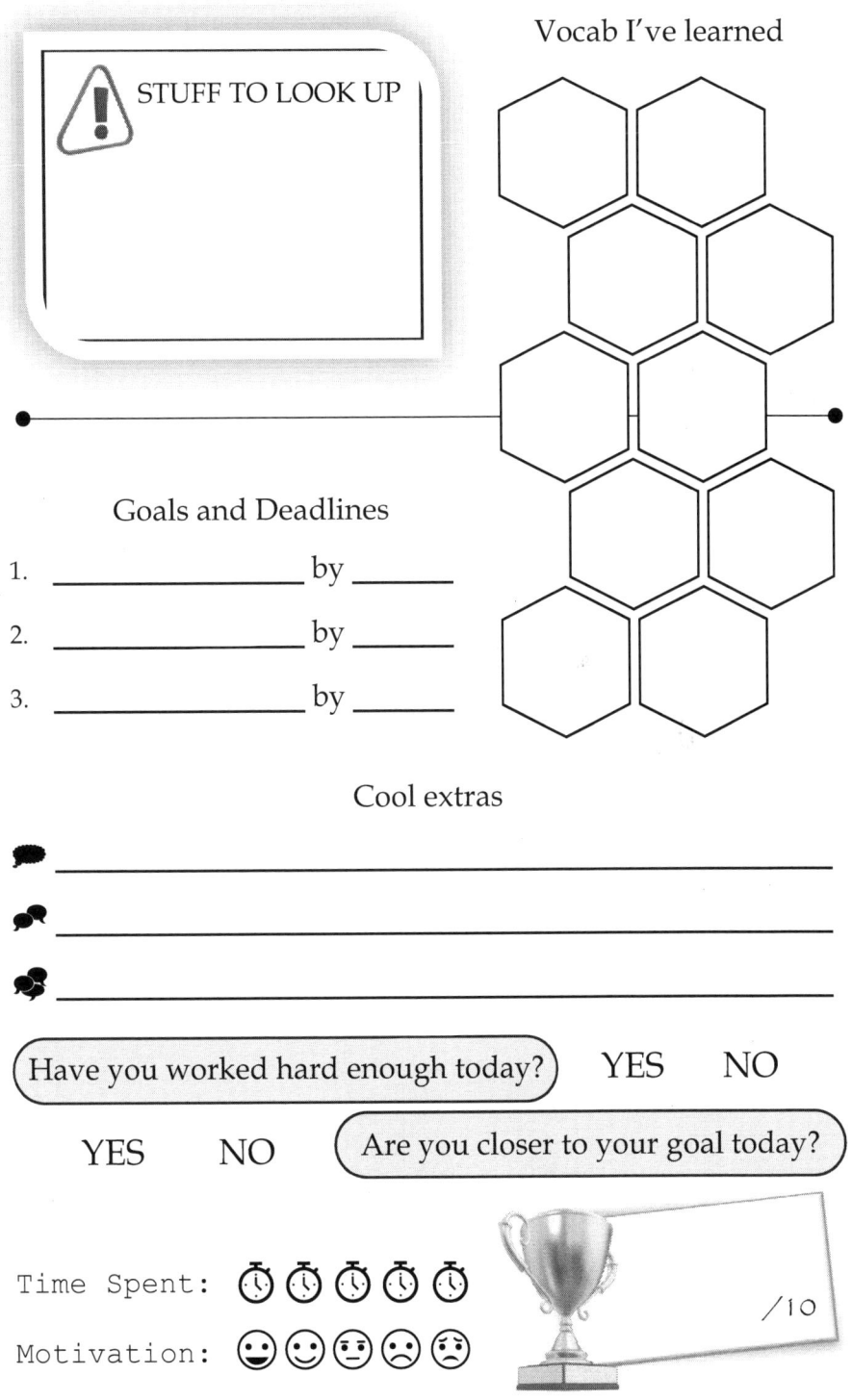

⚠ STUFF TO LOOK UP

Vocab I've learned

Goals and Deadlines

1. _____ by _____
2. _____ by _____
3. _____ by _____

Cool extras

💬 _____
💬 _____
💬 _____

(Have you worked hard enough today?)   YES   NO

YES   NO   (Are you closer to your goal today?)

Time Spent: ⏱ ⏱ ⏱ ⏱ ⏱

Motivation: 😀 🙂 😐 🙁 😟

/10

Learn a language, and you'll avoid a war
ARAB PROVERB

Today's work

Active Passive

☑ _____ ☐ ☐
☑ _____ ☐ ☐
☑ _____ ☐ ☐
☑ _____ ☐ ☐

Things I have memorized

• •
• •
• •

things I still can't remember

Season

Episode

Minute

!? Have you forced yourself today to speak the language with someone?   YES   NO

NOTES

_____
_____
_____

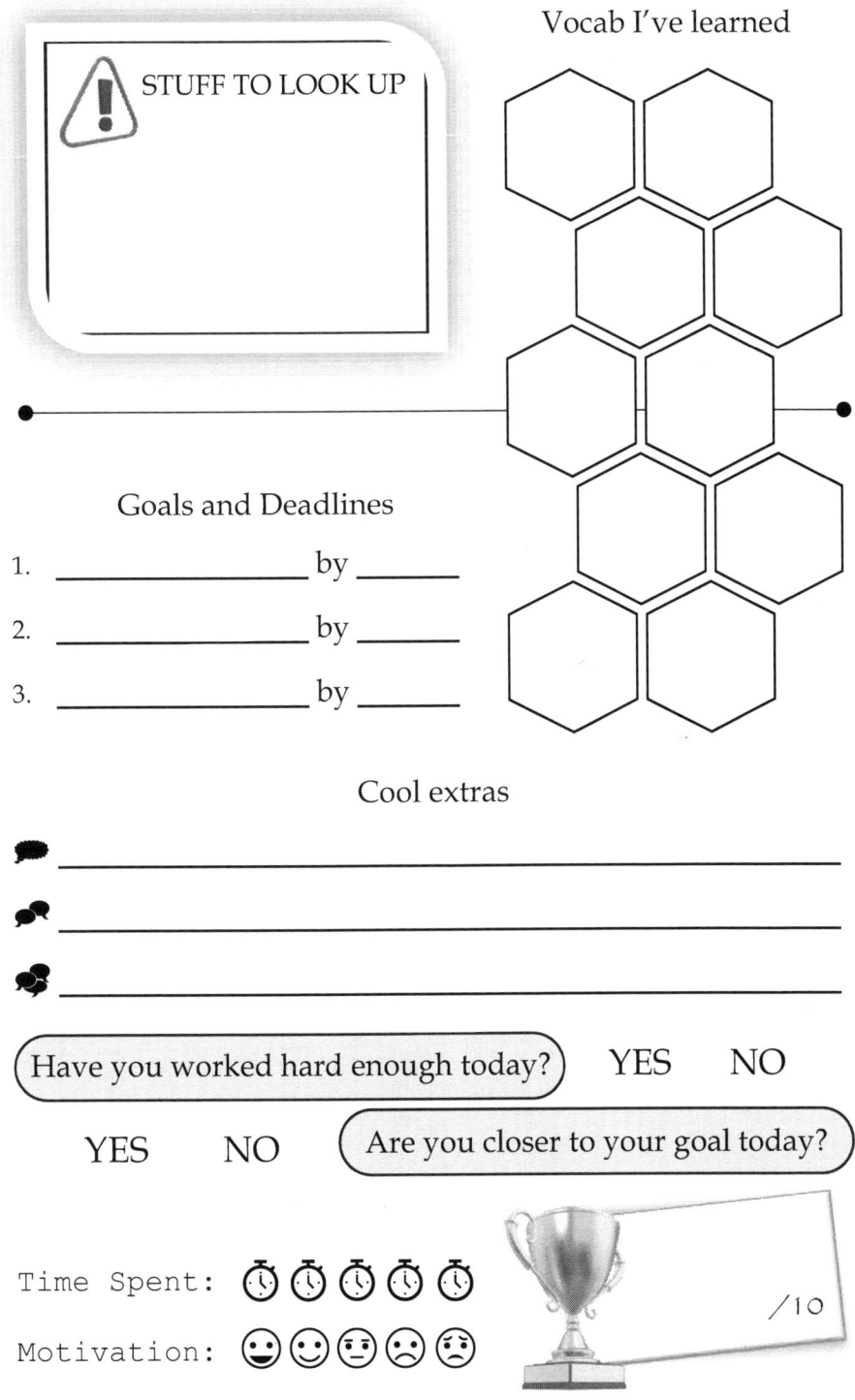

Language shapes the way we think, and determines what we can think about
BENJAMIN LEE WHORF

Today's work

Active Passive

☑ _____ ☐ ☐
☑ _____ ☐ ☐
☑ _____ ☐ ☐
☑ _____ ☐ ☐

Things I have memorized

• | •
• | •
• | •

things I still can't remember

Season

Episode

Minute

⁉ Have you forced yourself today to speak the language with someone?   YES   NO

NOTES

_____
_____
_____

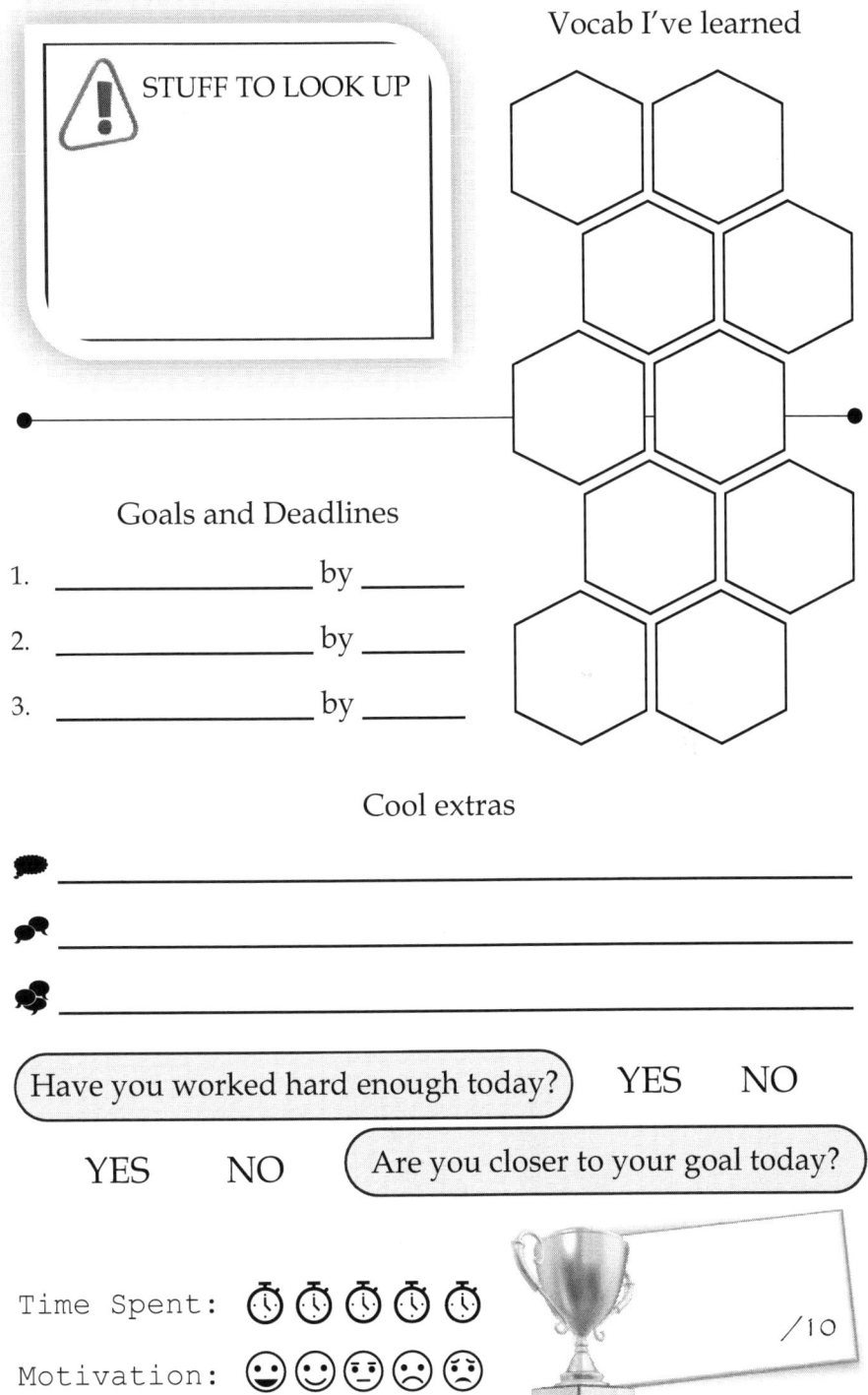

To have another language is to possess a second soul
CHARLEMAGNE

Today's work

Active Passive

☑ _____ ☐ ☐
☑ _____ ☐ ☐
☑ _____ ☐ ☐
☑ _____ ☐ ☐

Things I have memorized

things I still can't remember

Season

Episode

Minute

⁉ Have you forced yourself today to speak the language with someone?   YES   NO

NOTES

_____
_____
_____

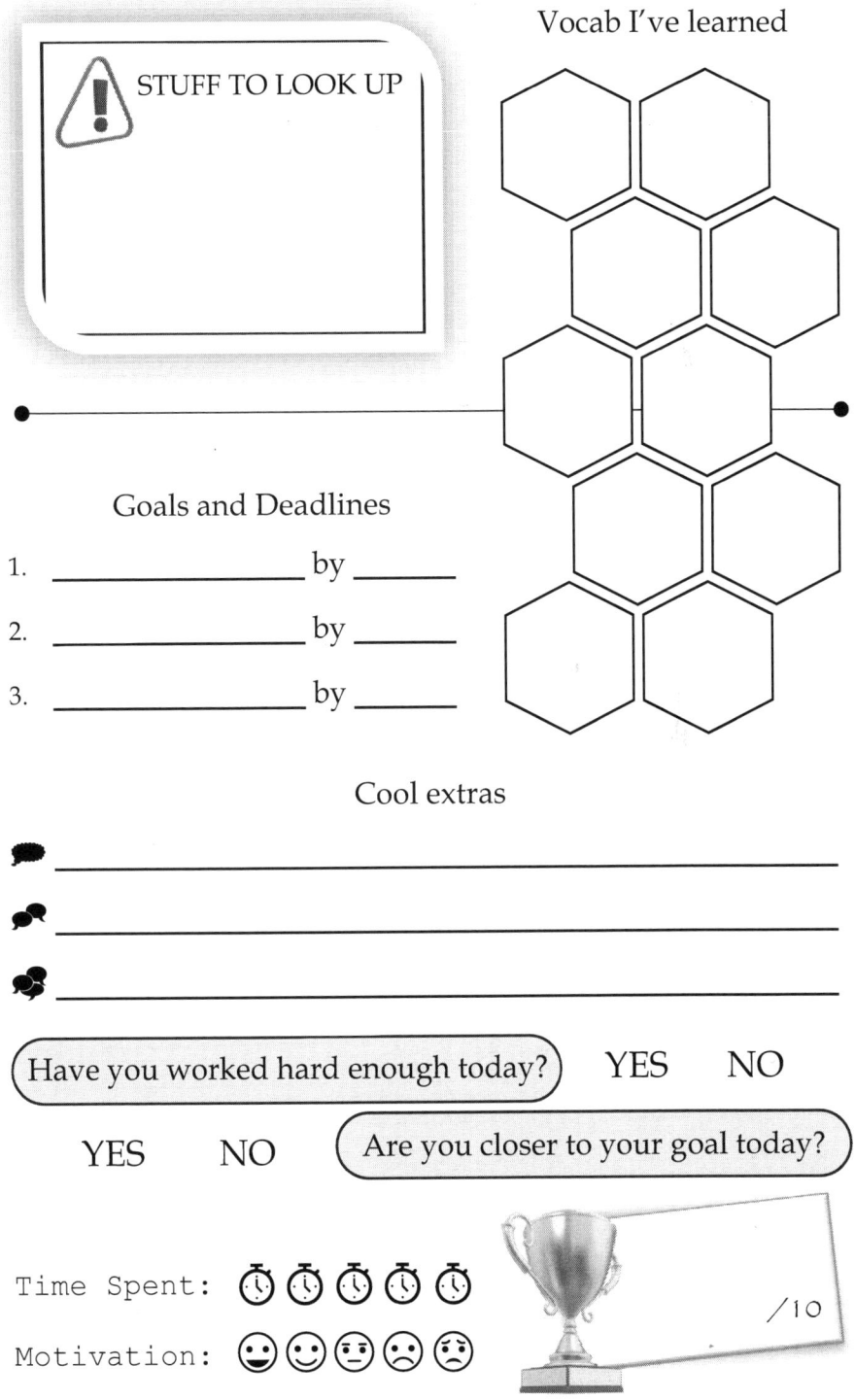

Learning is a treasure that will follow its owner everywhere
CHINESE PROVERB

Today's work

Active Passive

- ☑ _____ ☐ ☐
- ☑ _____ ☐ ☐
- ☑ _____ ☐ ☐
- ☑ _____ ☐ ☐

Things I have memorized

things I still can't remember

Season

Episode

Minute

!? Have you forced yourself today to speak the language with someone?   YES   NO

NOTES

_____
_____
_____

⚠ STUFF TO LOOK UP

Vocab I've learned

Goals and Deadlines

1. _____ by ____
2. _____ by ____
3. _____ by ____

Cool extras

🗨 _____
🗨 _____
🗨 _____

(Have you worked hard enough today?)   YES   NO

YES   NO   (Are you closer to your goal today?)

Time Spent: ⏱ ⏱ ⏱ ⏱ ⏱

Motivation: 😀 🙂 😐 🙁 😖

/10

All our dreams can come true if we have the courage to pursue them
WALT DISNEY

Today's work

Active Passive

☑ _____ ☐ ☐
☑ _____ ☐ ☐
☑ _____ ☐ ☐
☑ _____ ☐ ☐

Things I have memorized

things I still can't remember

Season

Episode

Minute

⁉ Have you forced yourself today to speak the language with someone?   YES   NO

NOTES

_____
_____
_____

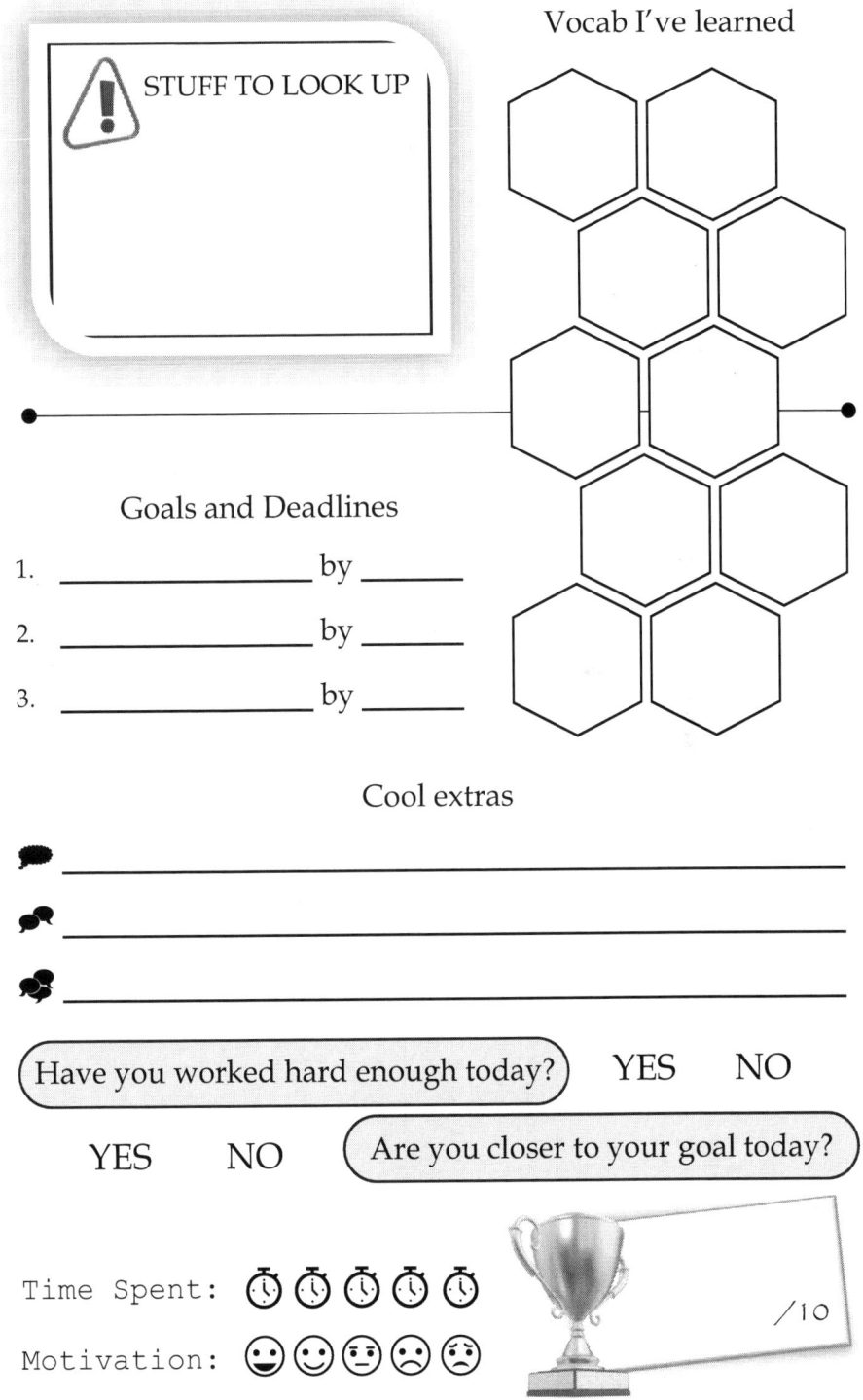

If you do what you always did, you will get what you always got
ANONYMOUS

Today's work

Active Passive

- ☑ _____ ☐ ☐
- ☑ _____ ☐ ☐
- ☑ _____ ☐ ☐
- ☑ _____ ☐ ☐

Things I have memorized

things I still can't remember

Season

Episode

Minute

⁉ Have you forced yourself today to speak the language with someone?   YES   NO

NOTES

_____

_____

_____

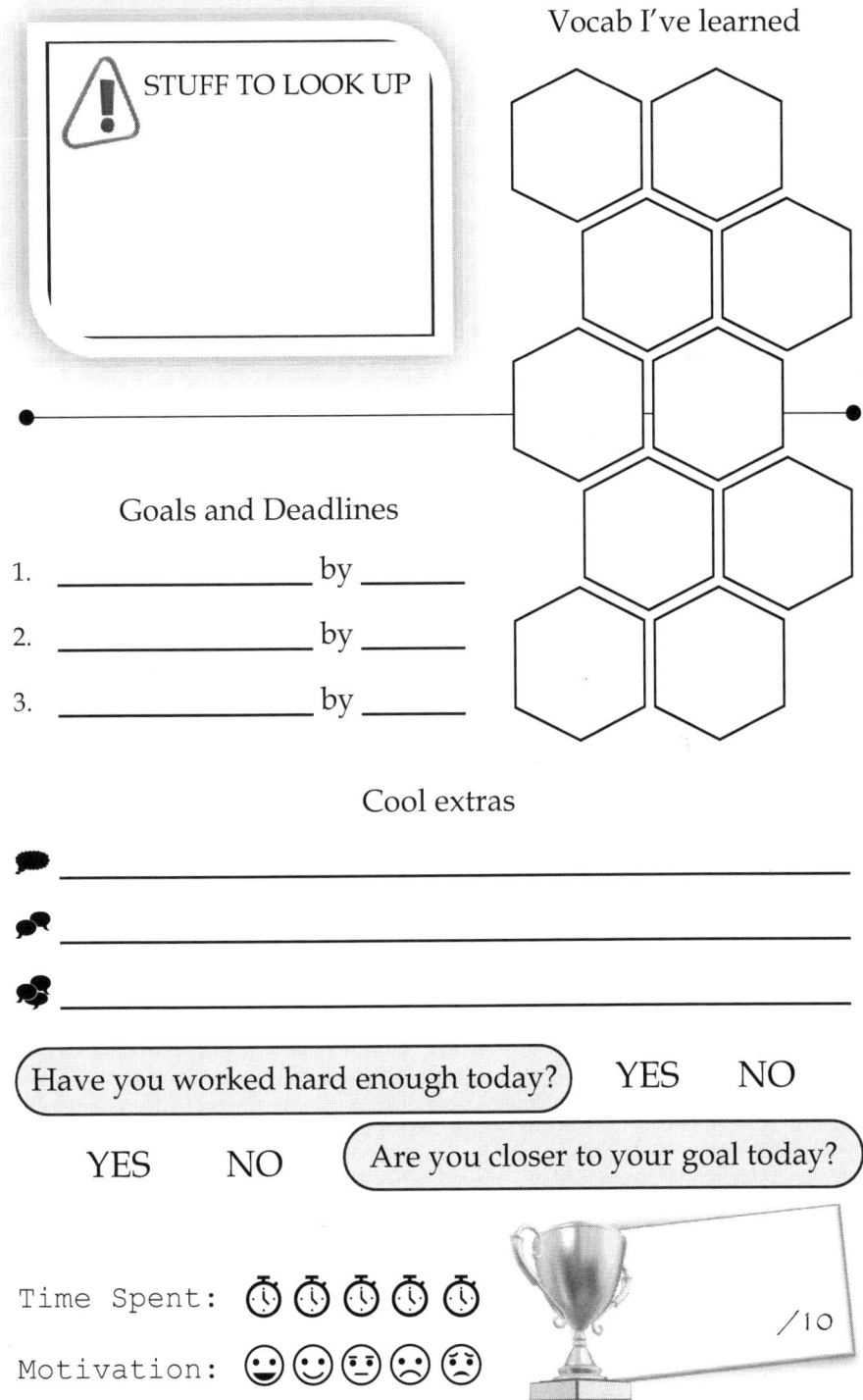

With languages, you are at home anywhere
EDWARD DE WAAL

Today's work

	Active	Passive
☑ _____	☐	☐
☑ _____	☐	☐
☑ _____	☐	☐
☑ _____	☐	☐

Things I have memorized

- •
- •
- •

things I still can't remember

Season
Episode
Minute

⁉ Have you forced yourself today to speak the language with someone?   YES   NO

NOTES

_____
_____
_____

⚠ STUFF TO LOOK UP

Vocab I've learned

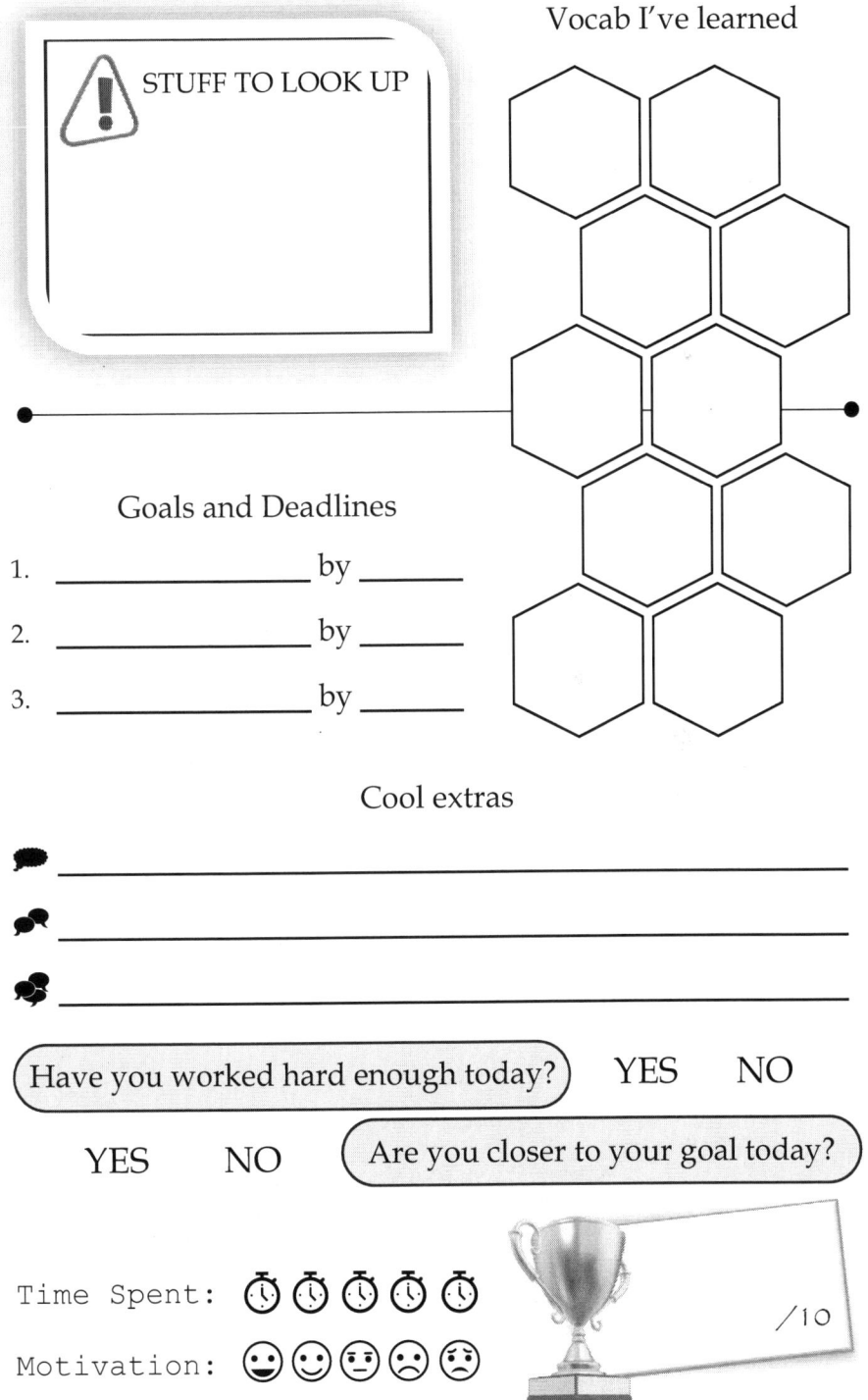

Goals and Deadlines

1. _____ by _____
2. _____ by _____
3. _____ by _____

Cool extras

🗨 _____
🗨 _____
🗨 _____

(Have you worked hard enough today?)   YES   NO

YES   NO   (Are you closer to your goal today?)

Time Spent: ⏱ ⏱ ⏱ ⏱ ⏱

Motivation: 😀 🙂 😐 🙁 😟

/10

A different language is a different vision of life
FEDERICO FELLINI

Today's work

Active Passive

☑ _____ ☐ ☐
☑ _____ ☐ ☐
☑ _____ ☐ ☐
☑ _____ ☐ ☐

Things I have memorized

things I still can't remember

Season
Episode
Minute

⁉ Have you forced yourself today to speak the language with someone?   YES   NO

NOTES

_____
_____
_____

⚠ STUFF TO LOOK UP

Vocab I've learned

Goals and Deadlines

1. _____ by _____
2. _____ by _____
3. _____ by _____

Cool extras

🗨 _____
🗨 _____
🗨 _____

(Have you worked hard enough today?)   YES   NO

YES   NO   (Are you closer to your goal today?)

Time Spent: ⏱ ⏱ ⏱ ⏱ ⏱

Motivation: 😀 🙂 😐 🙁 😟

/10

[36]

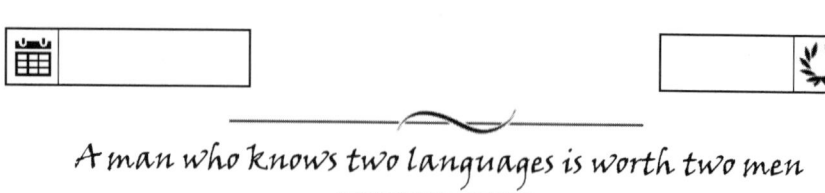

A man who knows two languages is worth two men
FRECH PROVERB

Today's work

Active Passive

☑ _____ ☐ ☐
☑ _____ ☐ ☐
☑ _____ ☐ ☐
☑ _____ ☐ ☐

Things I have memorized

things I still can't remember

Season

Episode

Minute

⁉ Have you forced yourself today to speak the language with someone?   YES   NO

NOTES

_____
_____
_____

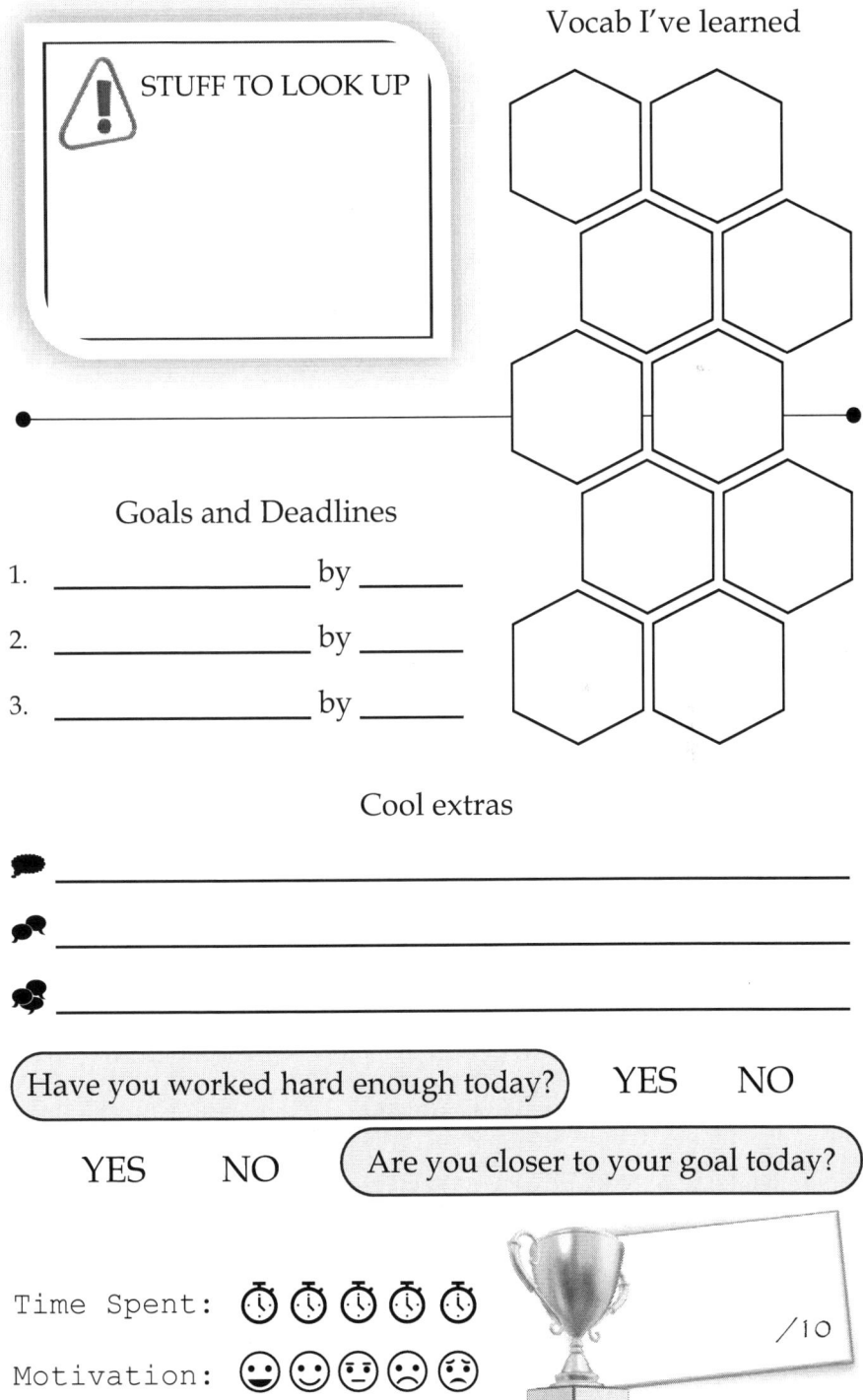

He who knows no foreign languages know nothing of his own
JOHANN WOLFGANG VON GOETHE

Today's work

Active Passive

☑ _____ ☐ ☐
☑ _____ ☐ ☐
☑ _____ ☐ ☐
☑ _____ ☐ ☐

Things I have memorized

things I still can't remember

Season
Episode
Minute

⁉ Have you forced yourself today to speak the language with someone?   YES   NO

NOTES

_____
_____
_____

⚠ STUFF TO LOOK UP

Vocab I've learned

Goals and Deadlines

1. _____ by _____
2. _____ by _____
3. _____ by _____

Cool extras

💬 _____
💬 _____
💬 _____

Have you worked hard enough today?   YES   NO

YES   NO   Are you closer to your goal today?

Time Spent: ⏱ ⏱ ⏱ ⏱ ⏱

Motivation: 😀 🙂 😐 🙁 😟

/10

📅 ☐☐☐☐☐☐☐☐☐ 🏅

Try not to become a person of success, but rather try to become a person of value
ALBERT EINSTEIN

Today's work

Active Passive

☑ _____ ☐ ☐
☑ _____ ☐ ☐
☑ _____ ☐ ☐
☑ _____ ☐ ☐

Things I have memorized

• | •
• | •
• | •

things I still can't remember

Season

Episode

Minute

‼️❓ Have you forced yourself today to speak the language with someone?   YES   NO

NOTES

_____
_____
_____

STUFF TO LOOK UP

Vocab I've learned

Goals and Deadlines

1. _____ by _____
2. _____ by _____
3. _____ by _____

Cool extras

- _____
- _____
- _____

Have you worked hard enough today? YES NO

YES NO Are you closer to your goal today?

Time Spent:
Motivation:

/10

Great minds discuss ideas; average minds discuss events; small minds discuss people
ELEANOR ROOSEVELT

Today's work

Active Passive

☑ _____ ☐ ☐
☑ _____ ☐ ☐
☑ _____ ☐ ☐
☑ _____ ☐ ☐

Things I have memorized

things I still can't remember

Season

Episode

Minute

⁉ Have you forced yourself today to speak the language with someone?   YES   NO

NOTES

_____
_____
_____

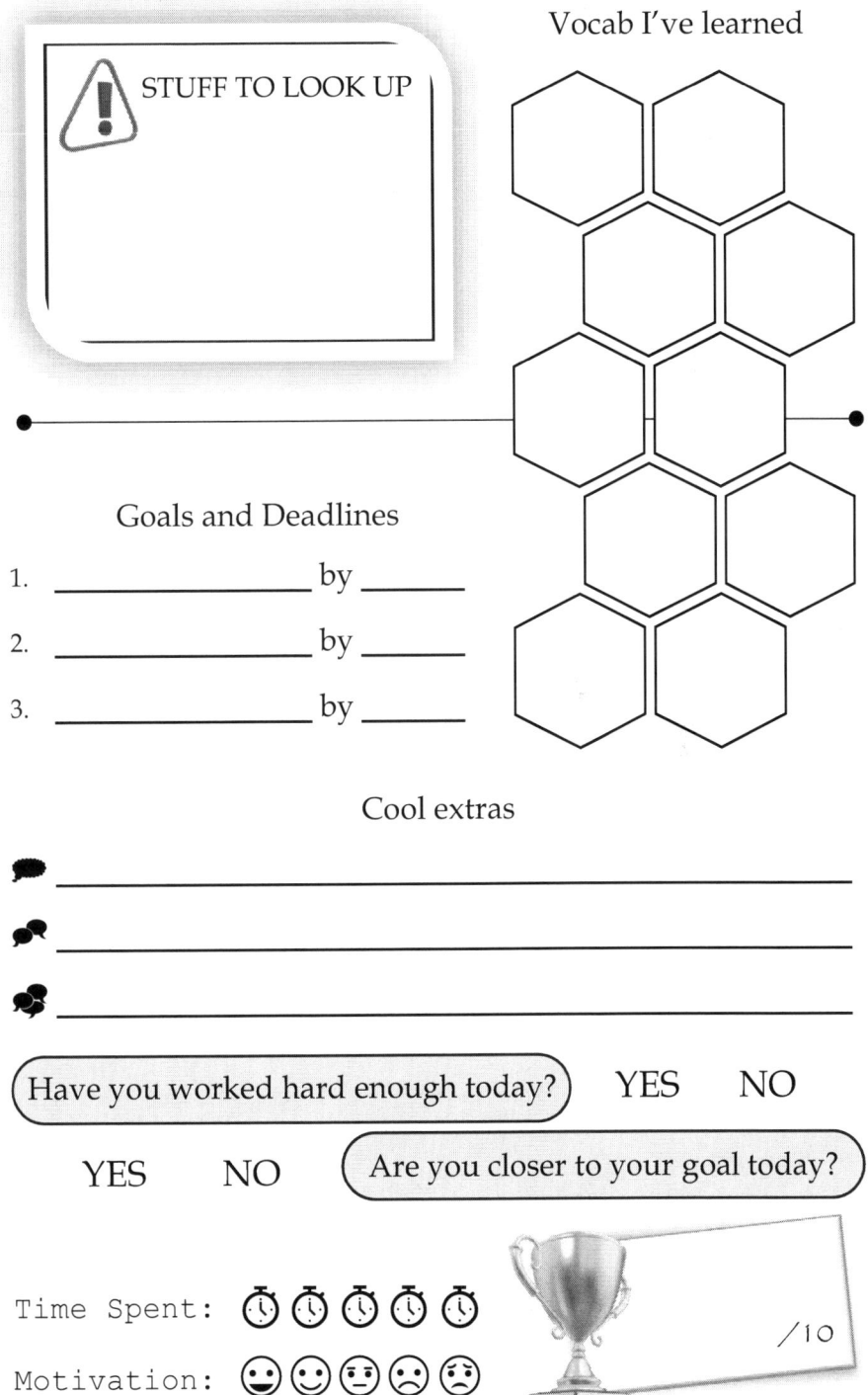

A new language is a new life
PERSIAN PROVERB

Today's work

Active Passive

- ☑ _____ ☐ ☐
- ☑ _____ ☐ ☐
- ☑ _____ ☐ ☐
- ☑ _____ ☐ ☐

Things I have memorized

things I still can't remember

Season

Episode

Minute

!? Have you forced yourself today to speak the language with someone?   YES   NO

NOTES

_____
_____
_____

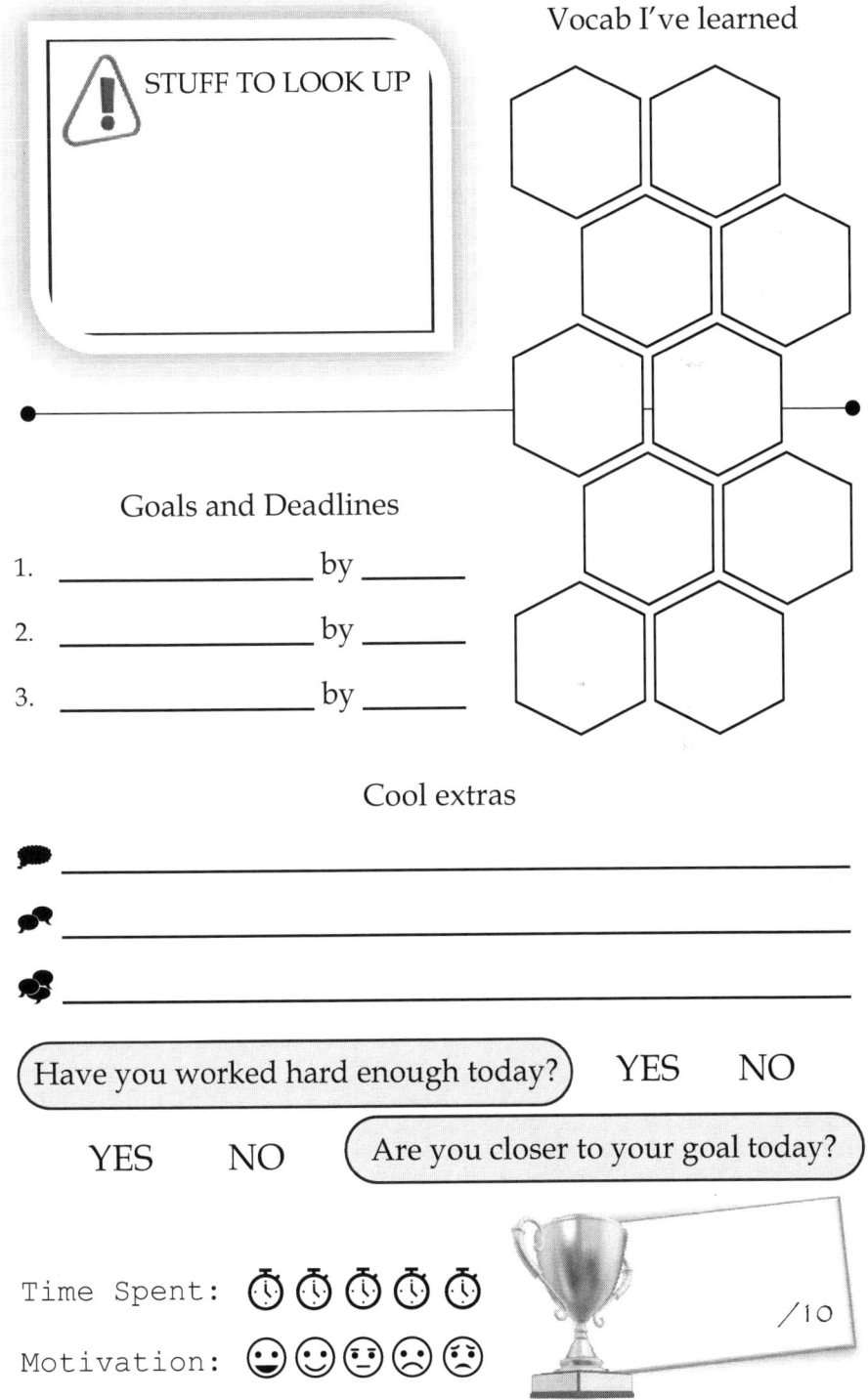

⚠ STUFF TO LOOK UP

Vocab I've learned

Goals and Deadlines

1. _____ by _____
2. _____ by _____
3. _____ by _____

Cool extras

🗨 _____
🗨 _____
🗨 _____

(Have you worked hard enough today?)　YES　NO

YES　NO　(Are you closer to your goal today?)

Time Spent: ⏱ ⏱ ⏱ ⏱ ⏱

Motivation: 😀 🙂 😐 🙁 😟

___/10

[46]

Knowledge of languages is the doorway to wisdom
ROGER BACON

Today's work

Active Passive

☑ _____ ☐ ☐
☑ _____ ☐ ☐
☑ _____ ☐ ☐
☑ _____ ☐ ☐

Things I have memorized

• •
• •
• •

things I still can't remember

Season
Episode
Minute

⁉ Have you forced yourself today to speak the language with someone?   YES   NO

NOTES

_____
_____
_____

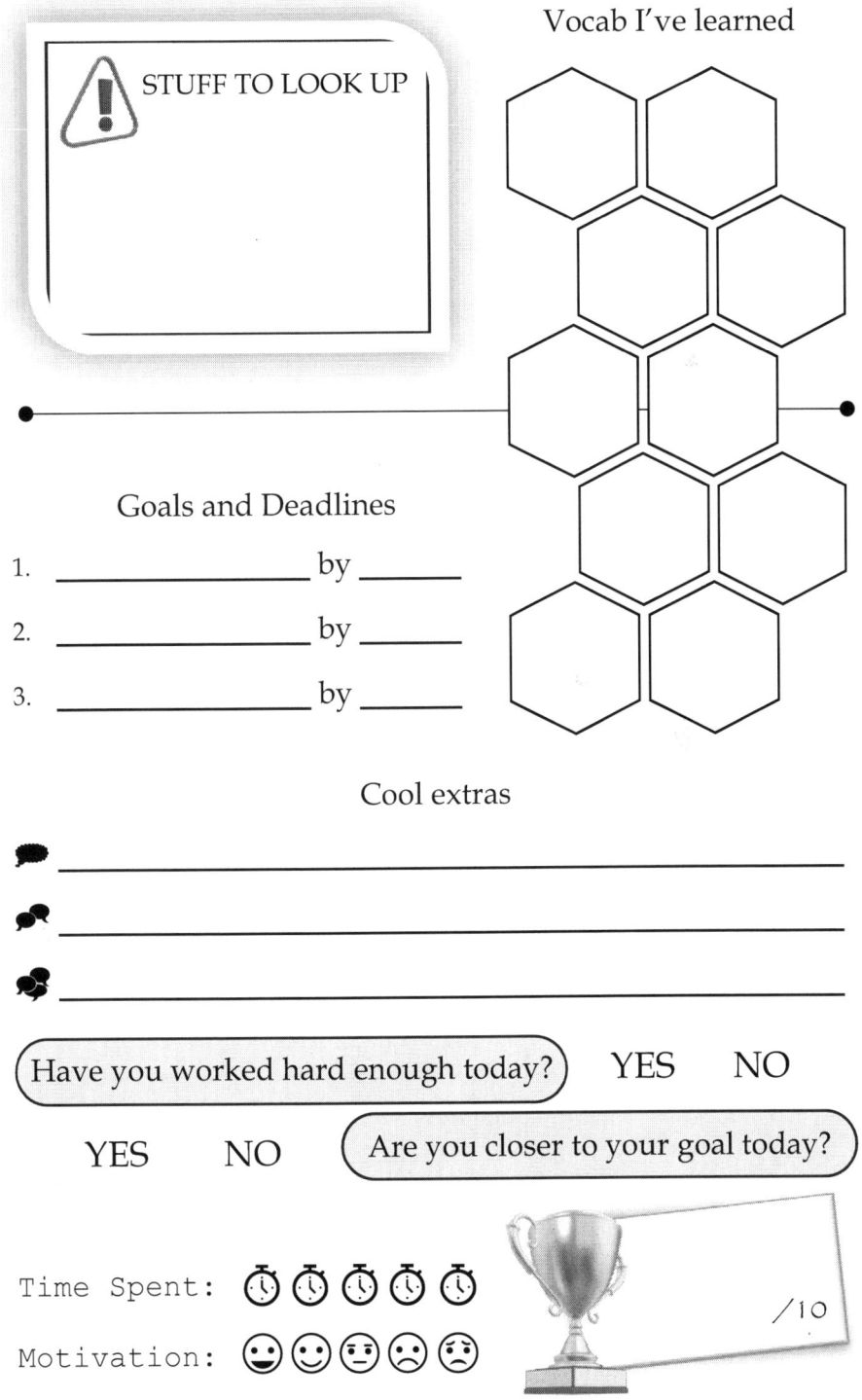

Language is wine upon the lips
VIRGINIA WOOLF

Today's work

Active Passive

- ☑ _____ ☐ ☐
- ☑ _____ ☐ ☐
- ☑ _____ ☐ ☐
- ☑ _____ ☐ ☐

Things I have memorized

things I still can't remember

Season

Episode

Minute

!? Have you forced yourself today to speak the language with someone?   YES   NO

NOTES

_____
_____
_____

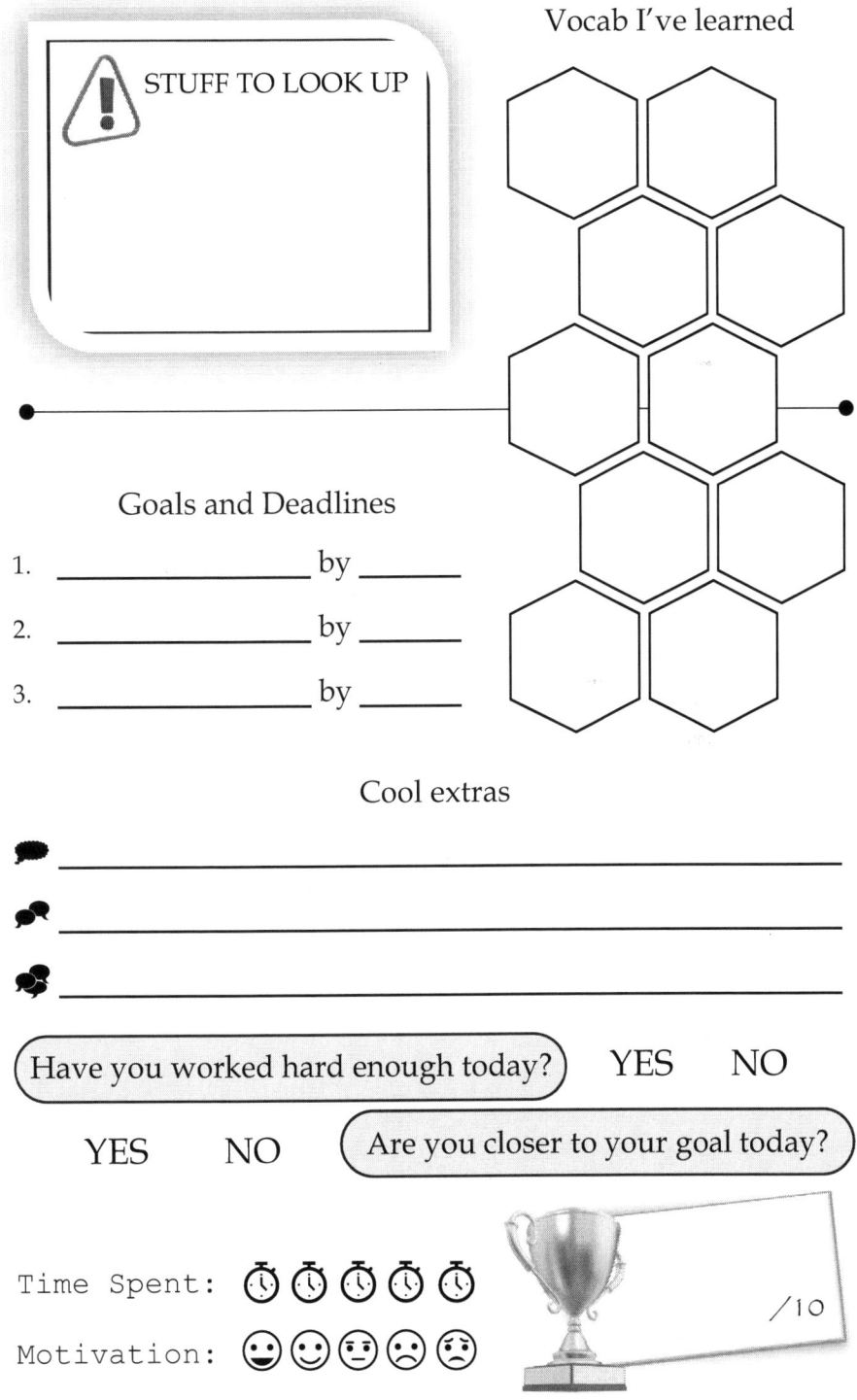

Language is to the mind more than light is to the eye
WILLIAM GIBSON

Today's work

Active Passive

- ☑ _____ ☐ ☐
- ☑ _____ ☐ ☐
- ☑ _____ ☐ ☐
- ☑ _____ ☐ ☐

Things I have memorized

things I still can't remember

Season
Episode
Minute

⁉ Have you forced yourself today to speak the language with someone?   YES   NO

NOTES

_____
_____
_____

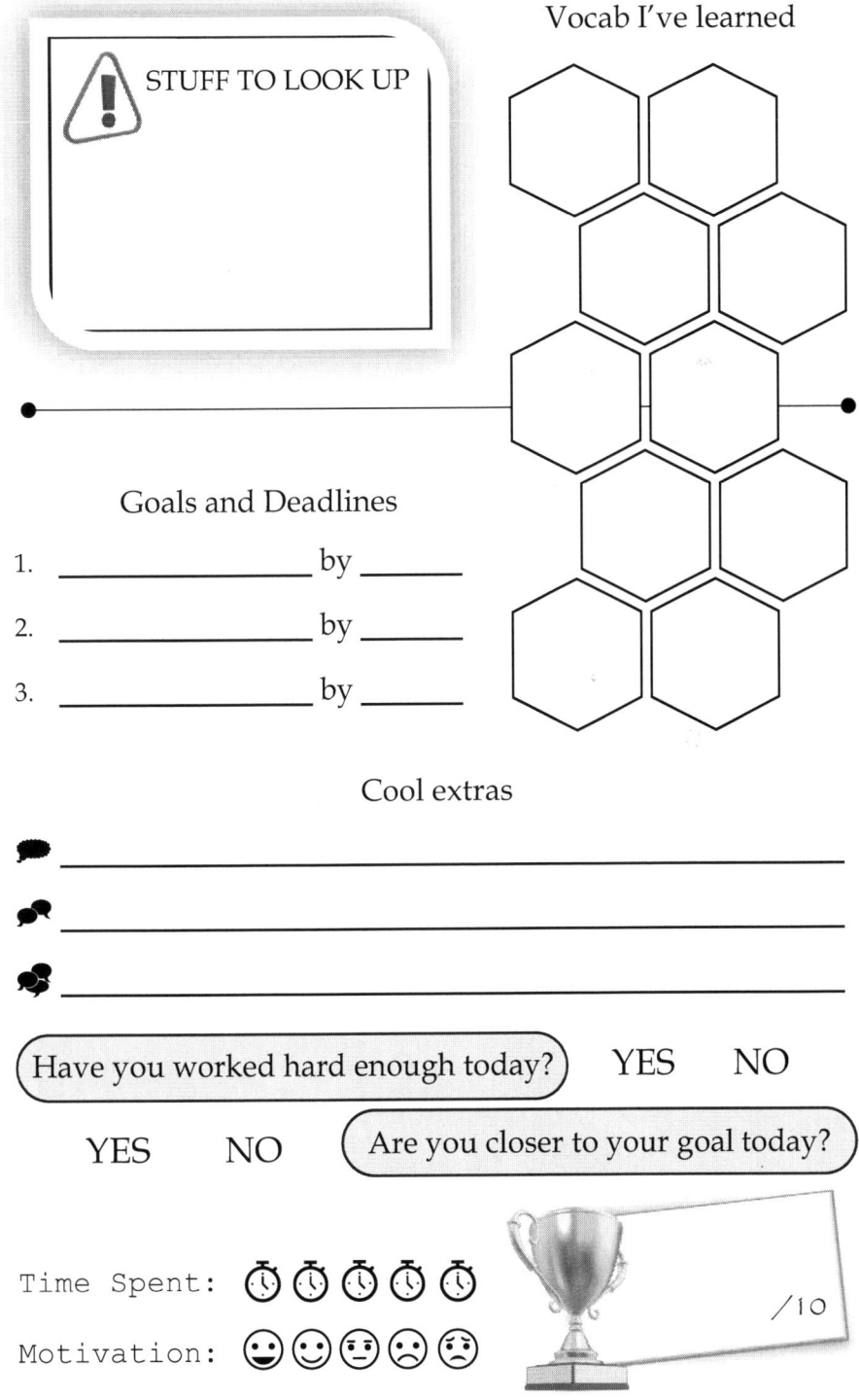

Old donkeys do not learn languages
PORTUGUESE PROVERB

Today's work
　　　　　　　　　　　　　　　　　　　　　Active　Passive

☑ _____ ☐ ☐
☑ _____ ☐ ☐
☑ _____ ☐ ☐
☑ _____ ☐ ☐

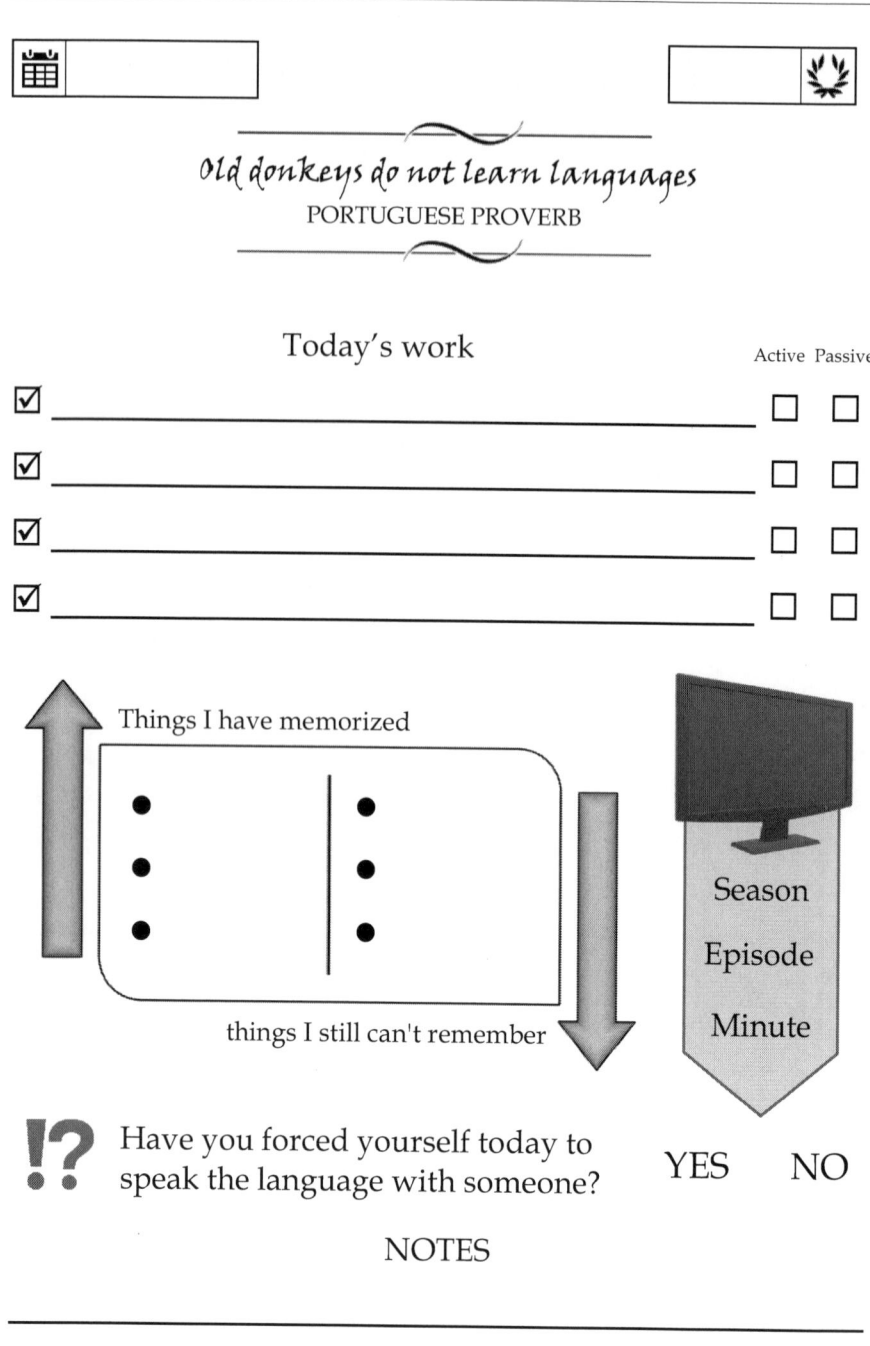

⁉ Have you forced yourself today to speak the language with someone?　YES　NO

NOTES

_____
_____
_____

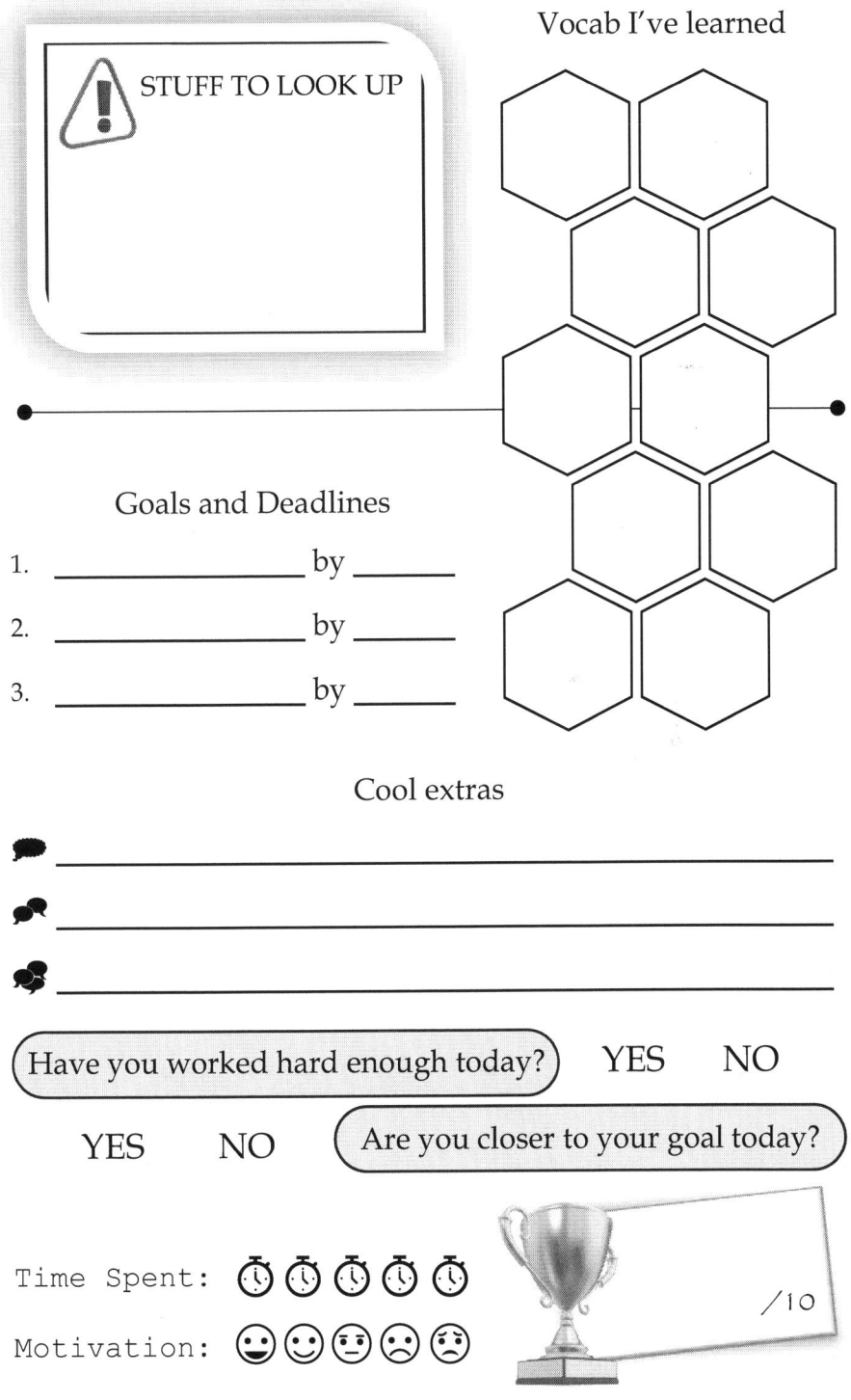

[54]

A man can be recognized by his language
JEWISH PROVERB

Today's work

Active Passive
- ☑ _____ ☐ ☐
- ☑ _____ ☐ ☐
- ☑ _____ ☐ ☐
- ☑ _____ ☐ ☐

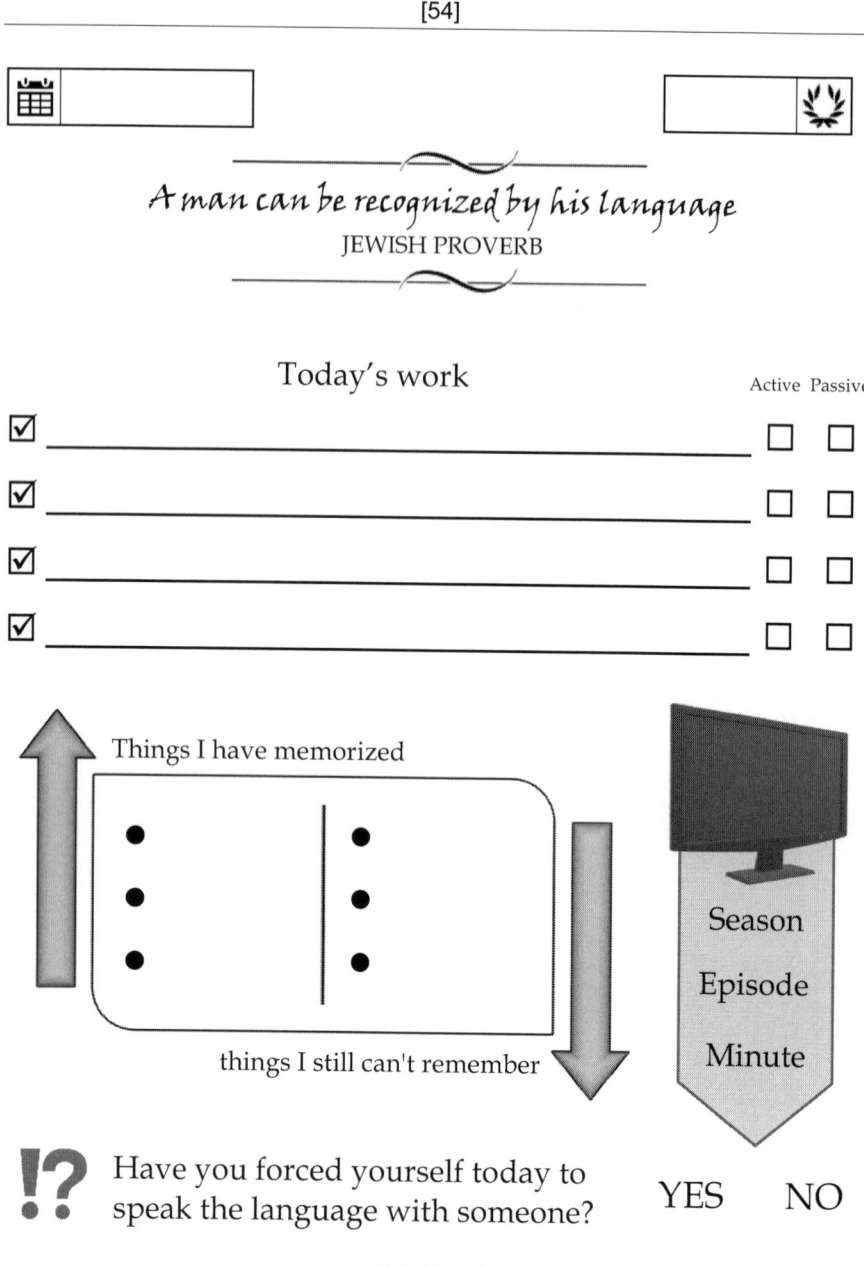

Things I have memorized

things I still can't remember

Season

Episode

Minute

⁉ Have you forced yourself today to speak the language with someone?   YES   NO

NOTES

_____

_____

_____

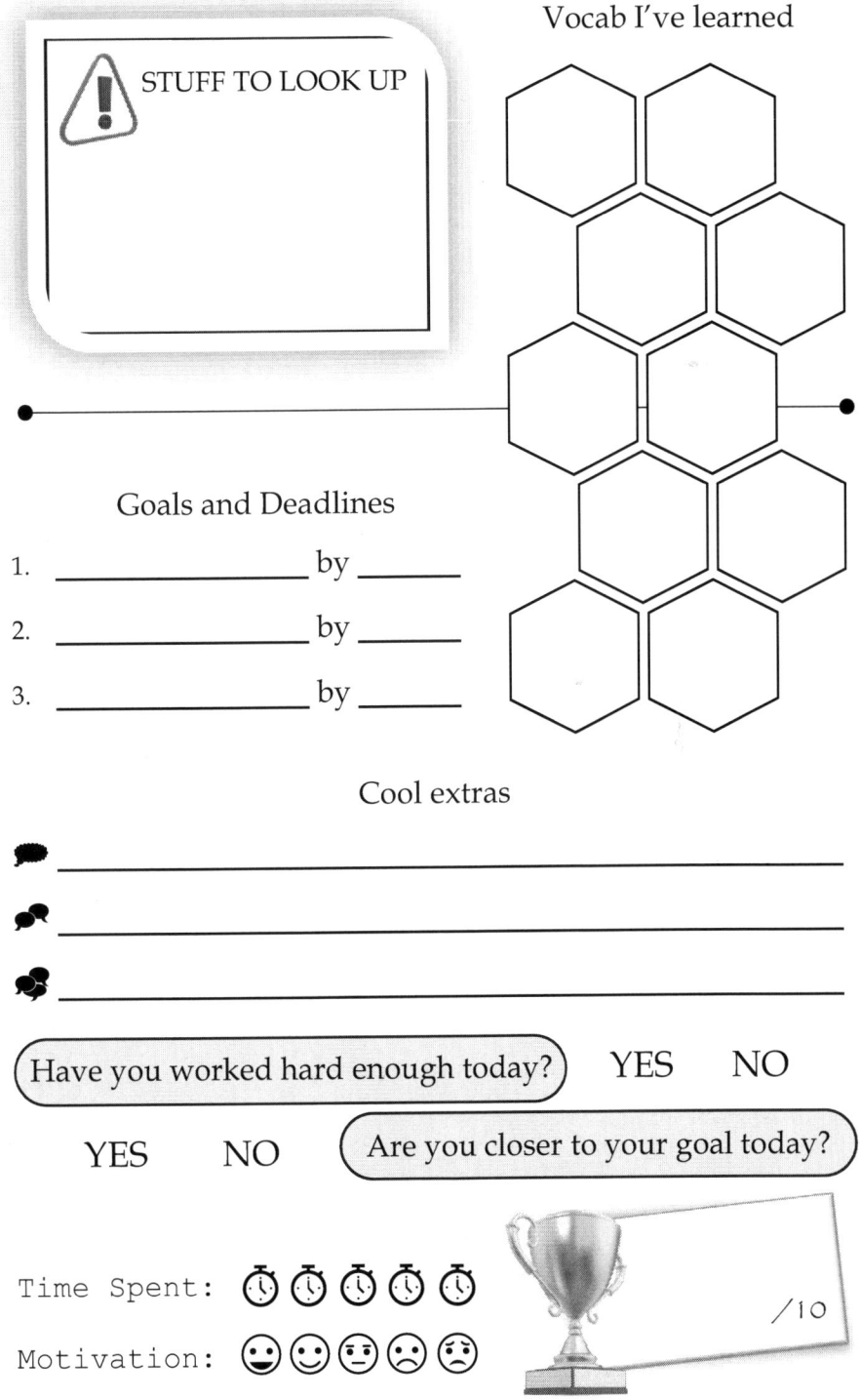

Language is the archives of history
RALPH WALDO EMERSON

Today's work   Active Passive

☑ _____ ☐ ☐
☑ _____ ☐ ☐
☑ _____ ☐ ☐
☑ _____ ☐ ☐

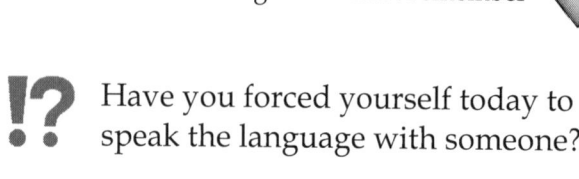

Season

Episode

Minute

⁉ Have you forced yourself today to speak the language with someone?   YES   NO

NOTES

_____
_____
_____

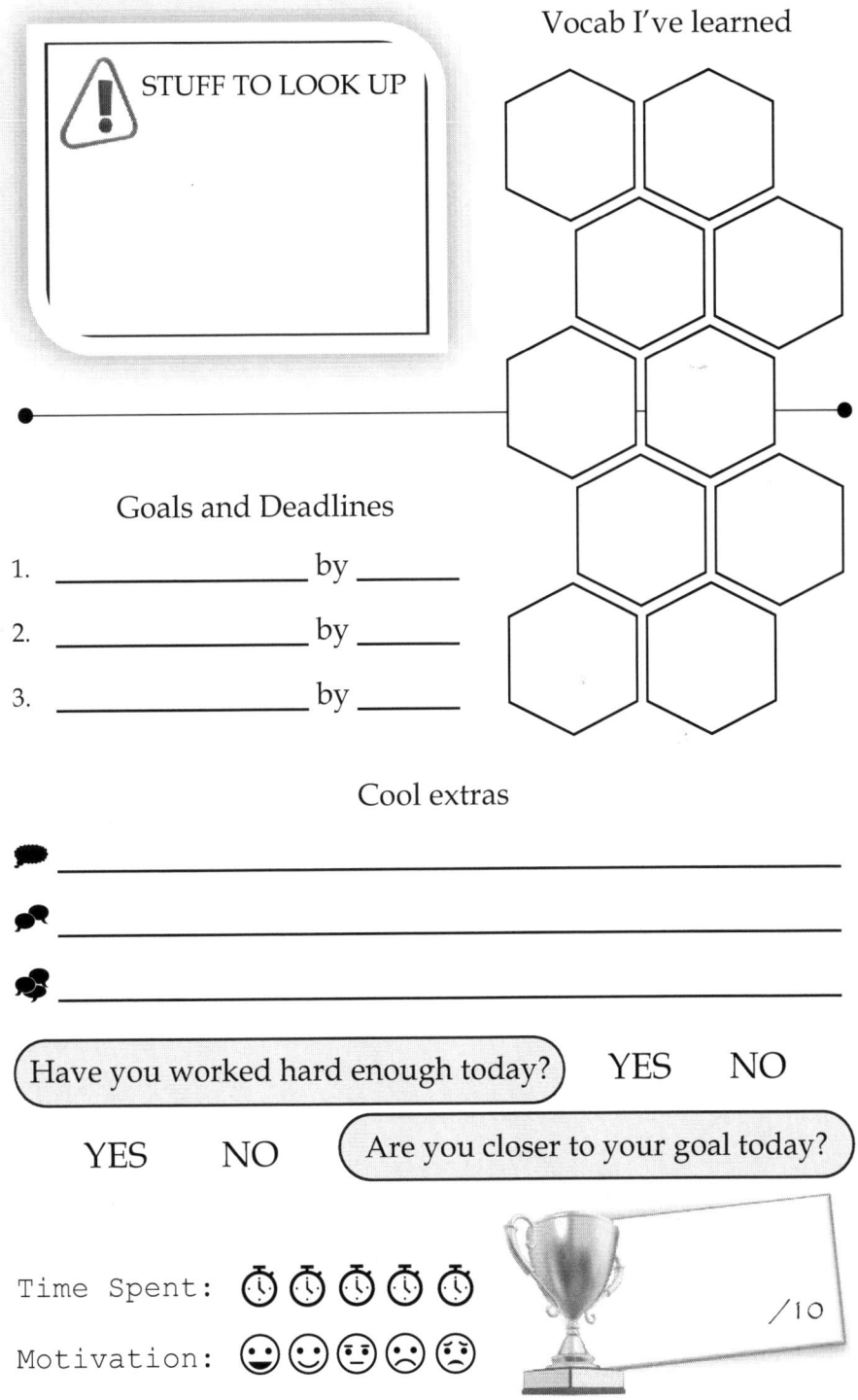

No masterpiece was ever created by a lazy artist
ANONYMOUS

Today's work

Active   Passive

- ☑ _____ ☐ ☐
- ☑ _____ ☐ ☐
- ☑ _____ ☐ ☐
- ☑ _____ ☐ ☐

Things I have memorized

things I still can't remember

Season

Episode

Minute

⁉ Have you forced yourself today to speak the language with someone?   YES   NO

NOTES

_____

_____

_____

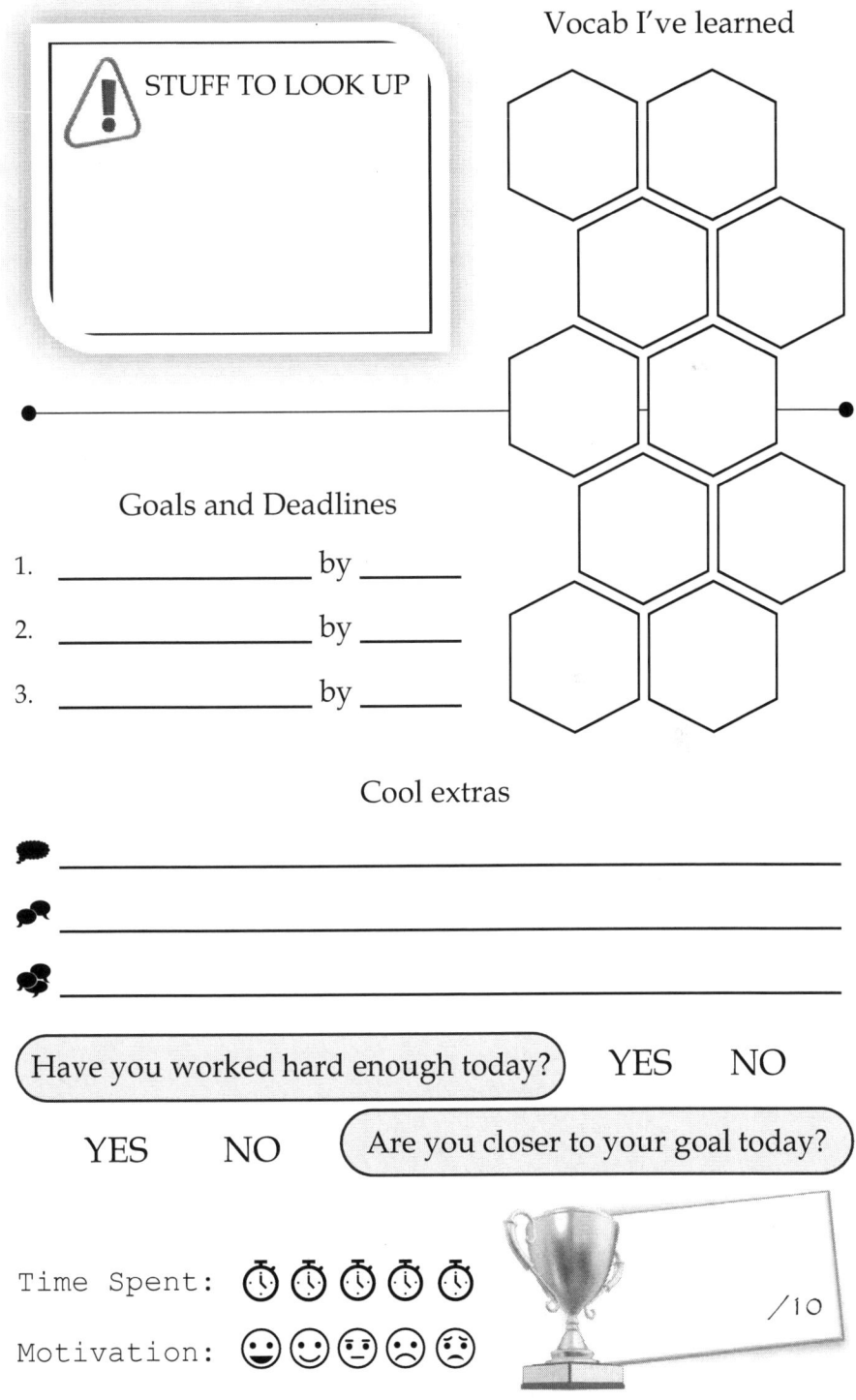

To learn a language: Use it or lose it. Love it or leave it. Feel it or fail it
SAFIR KASSIM BOUDJELAL

Today's work

Active Passive

- ☑ _____ ☐ ☐
- ☑ _____ ☐ ☐
- ☑ _____ ☐ ☐
- ☑ _____ ☐ ☐

Things I have memorized

things I still can't remember

Season

Episode

Minute

⁉ Have you forced yourself today to speak the language with someone?   YES   NO

NOTES

_____
_____
_____

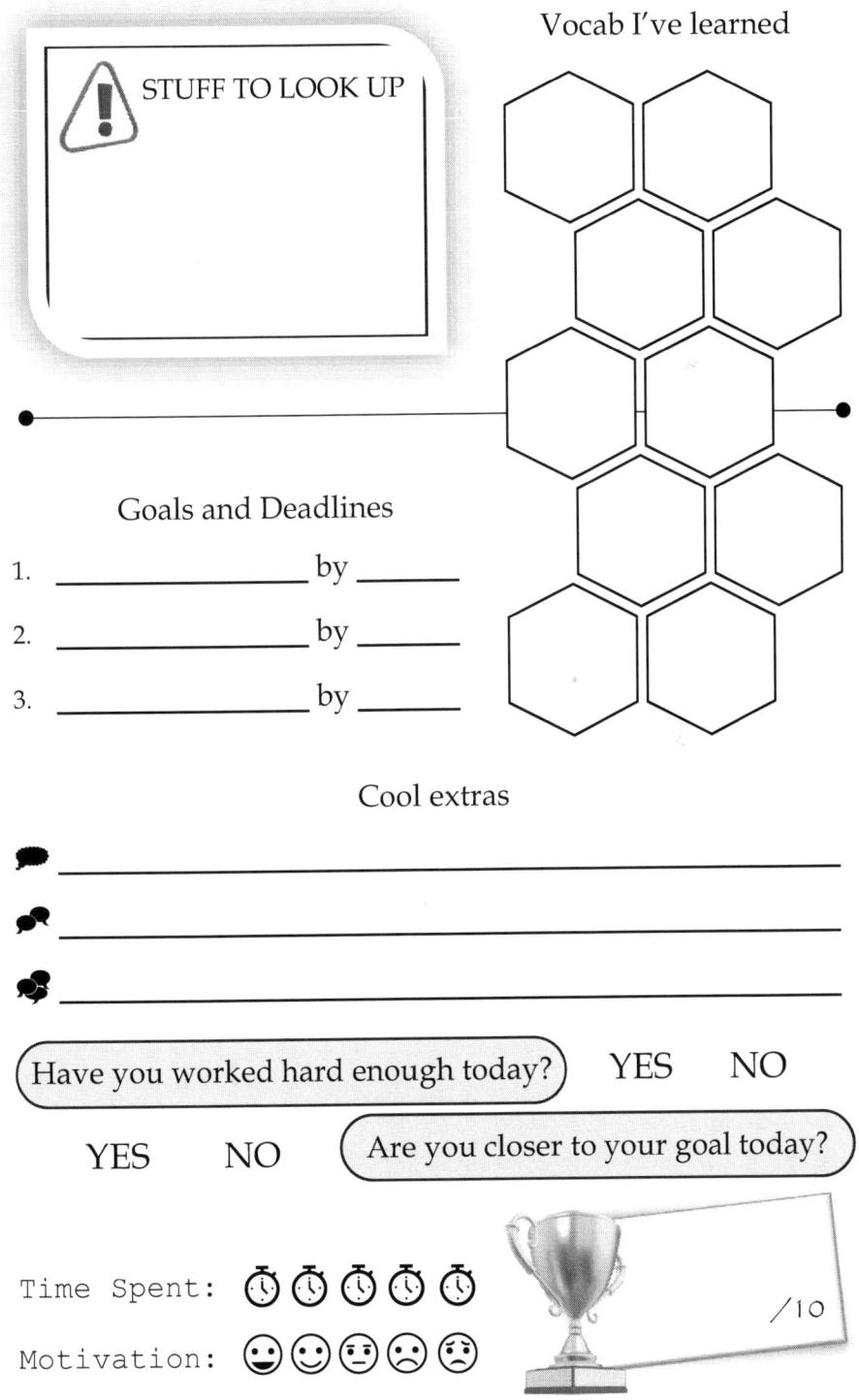

Do one thing every day that scares you in the language you are learning
ANONYMOUS

Today's work

Active Passive

- ☑ _____ ☐ ☐
- ☑ _____ ☐ ☐
- ☑ _____ ☐ ☐
- ☑ _____ ☐ ☐

Things I have memorized

things I still can't remember

Season

Episode

Minute

⁉ Have you forced yourself today to speak the language with someone?   YES   NO

NOTES
_____
_____
_____

⚠️ STUFF TO LOOK UP

Vocab I've learned

Goals and Deadlines

1. _____ by _____
2. _____ by _____
3. _____ by _____

Cool extras

💬 _____
💬 _____
💬 _____

Have you worked hard enough today? YES   NO

YES   NO   Are you closer to your goal today?

Time Spent: ⏱ ⏱ ⏱ ⏱ ⏱

Motivation: 😀 🙂 😐 🙁 😟

/10

Life is not about finding yourself. Life is about creating yourself
LOLLY DASKAL

Today's work

Active Passive

- [x] _____ ☐ ☐
- [x] _____ ☐ ☐
- [x] _____ ☐ ☐
- [x] _____ ☐ ☐

Things I have memorized

things I still can't remember

Season

Episode

Minute

!? Have you forced yourself today to speak the language with someone?   YES   NO

NOTES
_____
_____
_____

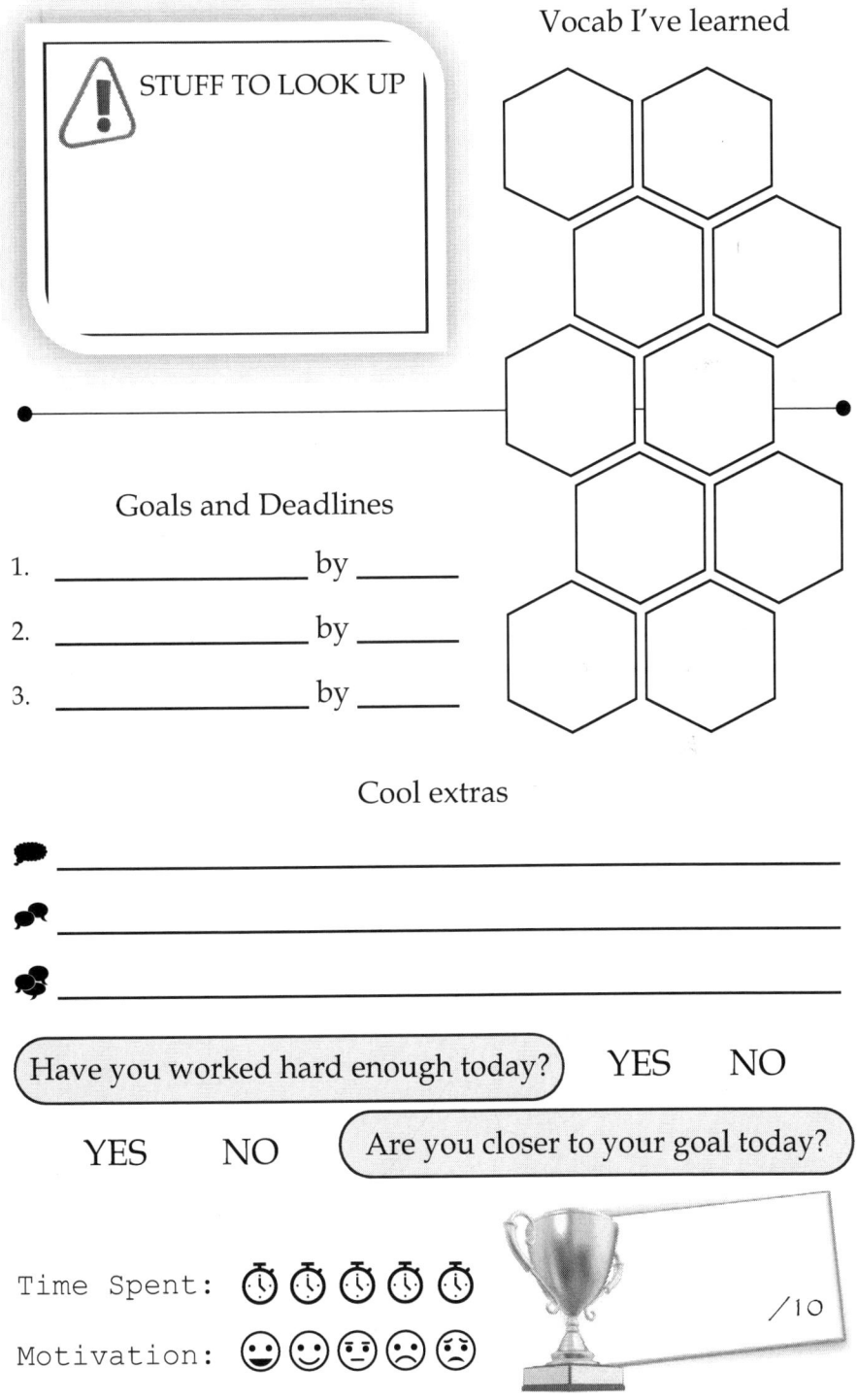

You can never understand one language until you understand at least two
GEOFFREY WILLIANS

Today's work

Active Passive

☑ _____ ☐ ☐
☑ _____ ☐ ☐
☑ _____ ☐ ☐
☑ _____ ☐ ☐

Things I have memorized

• •
• •
• •

things I still can't remember

Season

Episode

Minute

‼❓ Have you forced yourself today to speak the language with someone?   YES   NO

NOTES

_____

_____

_____

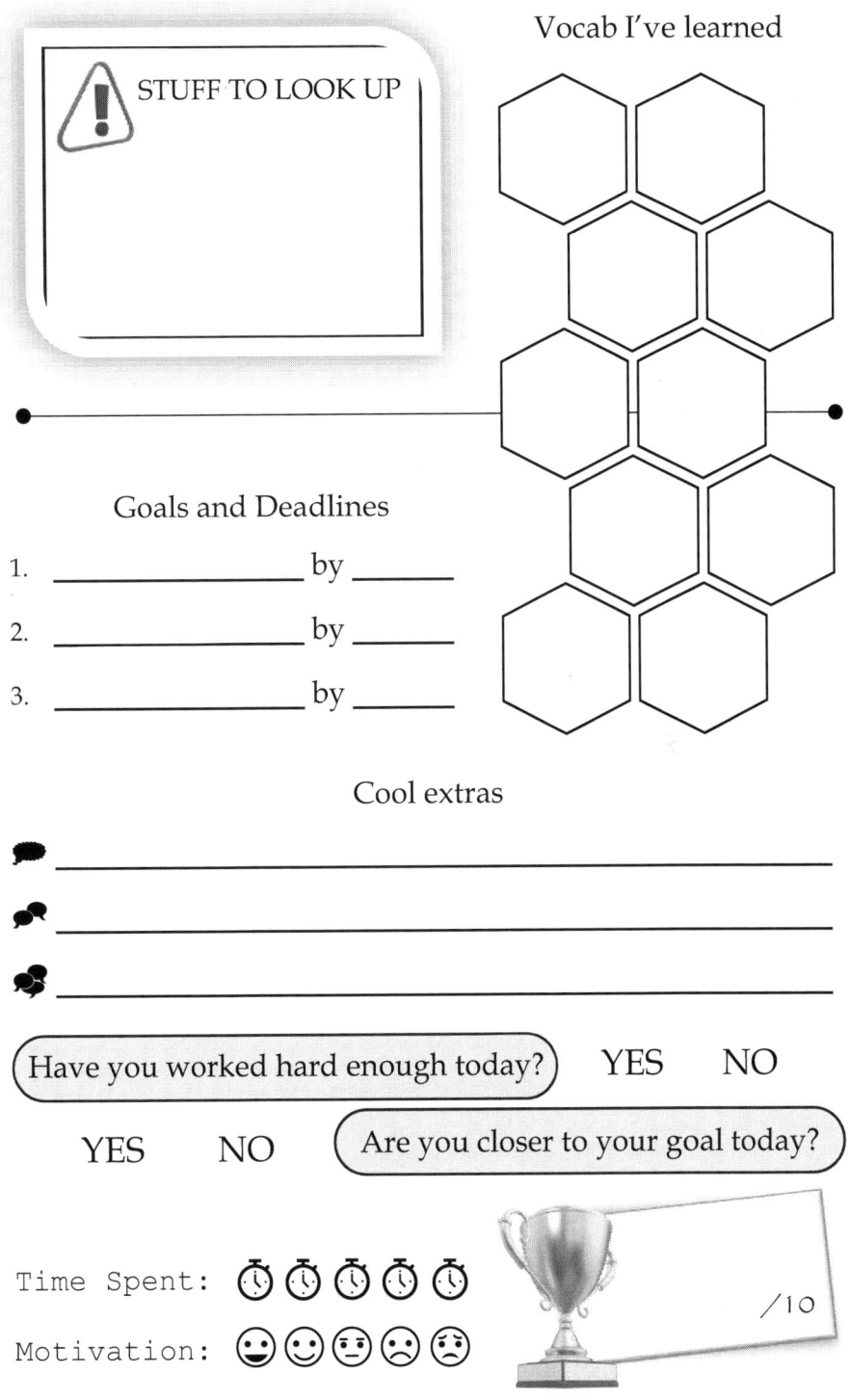

[68]

Speak a new language so that the world will be a new world
RUMI

Today's work

Active Passive

- ☑ _____ ☐ ☐
- ☑ _____ ☐ ☐
- ☑ _____ ☐ ☐
- ☑ _____ ☐ ☐

Things I have memorized

• | •
• | •
• | •

things I still can't remember

Season

Episode

Minute

⚠️ Have you forced yourself today to speak the language with someone?   YES   NO

NOTES

_____
_____
_____

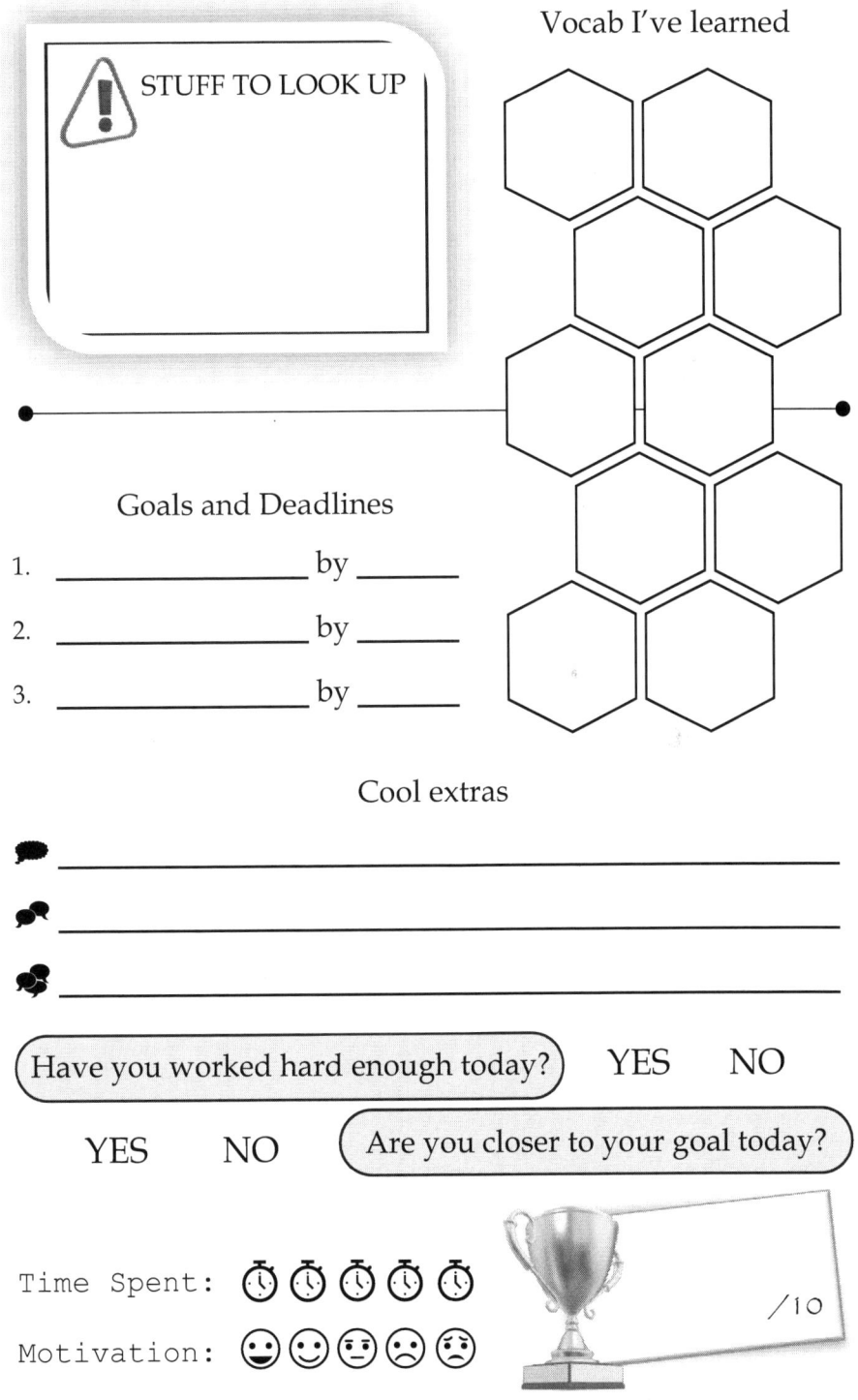

 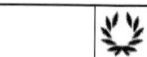

Any fool can know. The point is to understand
ALBERT EINSTEIN

Today's work

Active Passive

☑ _____ ☐ ☐
☑ _____ ☐ ☐
☑ _____ ☐ ☐
☑ _____ ☐ ☐

Things I have memorized

things I still can't remember

Season

Episode

Minute

⁉ Have you forced yourself today to speak the language with someone?   YES   NO

NOTES

_____
_____
_____

STUFF TO LOOK UP

Vocab I've learned

Goals and Deadlines

1. _____ by _____
2. _____ by _____
3. _____ by _____

Cool extras

💬 _____
💬 _____
💬 _____

Have you worked hard enough today?   YES   NO

YES   NO   Are you closer to your goal today?

Time Spent: ⏱ ⏱ ⏱ ⏱ ⏱

Motivation: 😀 🙂 😐 🙁 😣

/10

I find that the harder I work, the more luck I seem to have
THOMAS JEFFERSON

Today's work

Active Passive

☑ _____ ☐ ☐
☑ _____ ☐ ☐
☑ _____ ☐ ☐
☑ _____ ☐ ☐

Things I have memorized

• •
• •
• •

things I still can't remember

Season
Episode
Minute

⁉ Have you forced yourself today to speak the language with someone?   YES   NO

NOTES

_____
_____
_____

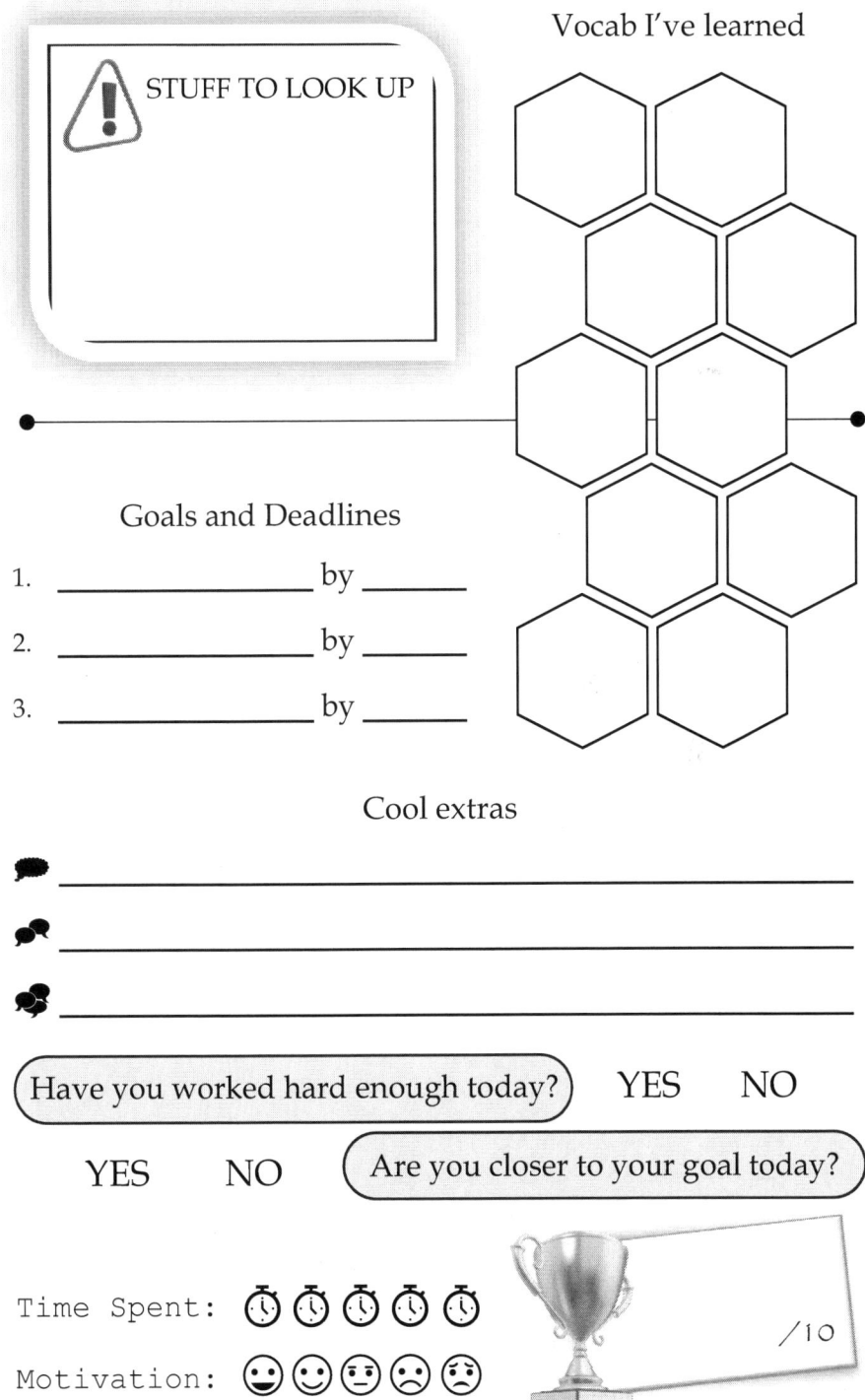

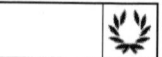

The starting point of all achievement is desire
NAPOLEON HILL

Today's work

Active Passive

☑ _____ ☐ ☐
☑ _____ ☐ ☐
☑ _____ ☐ ☐
☑ _____ ☐ ☐

Things I have memorized

• •
• •
• •

things I still can't remember

Season

Episode

Minute

!? Have you forced yourself today to speak the language with someone?   YES   NO

NOTES

_____
_____
_____

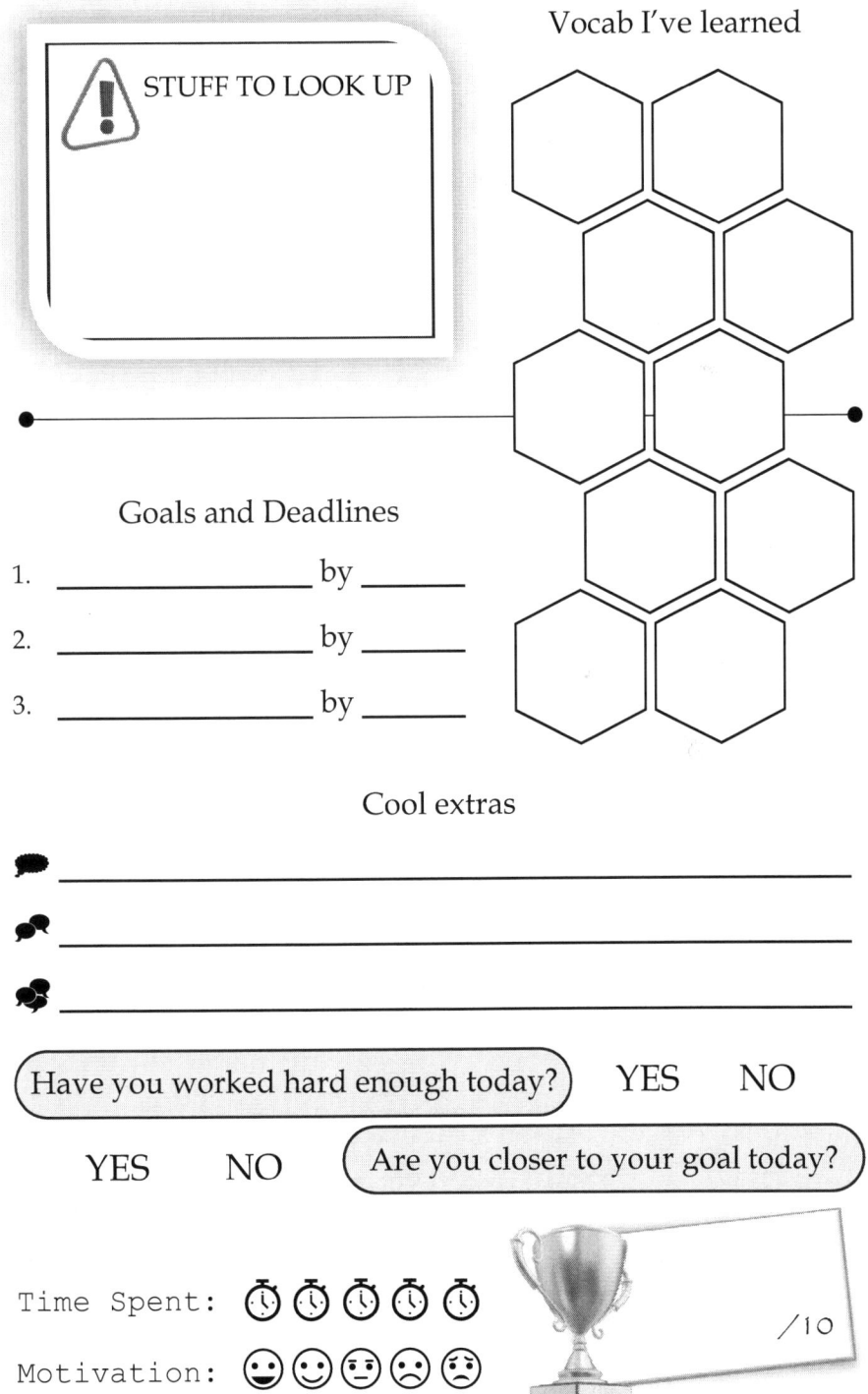

Success is the sum of small efforts, repeated day-in and day-out
ROBERT COLLIER

Today's work

Active Passive

- [x] _____ ☐ ☐
- [x] _____ ☐ ☐
- [x] _____ ☐ ☐
- [x] _____ ☐ ☐

Things I have memorized

things I still can't remember

Season

Episode

Minute

!? Have you forced yourself today to speak the language with someone?   YES   NO

NOTES

_____

_____

_____

⚠ STUFF TO LOOK UP

Vocab I've learned

Goals and Deadlines

1. _____ by _____
2. _____ by _____
3. _____ by _____

Cool extras

💬 _____
💬 _____
💬 _____

(Have you worked hard enough today?)   YES   NO

YES   NO   (Are you closer to your goal today?)

Time Spent: ⏱ ⏱ ⏱ ⏱ ⏱

Motivation: 😃 🙂 😐 🙁 😣

/10

All progress takes place outside the comfort zone
MICHAEL JOHN BOBAK

Today's work

Active Passive

- ☑ _____ ☐ ☐
- ☑ _____ ☐ ☐
- ☑ _____ ☐ ☐
- ☑ _____ ☐ ☐

Things I have memorized

things I still can't remember

Season

Episode

Minute

⁉ Have you forced yourself today to speak the language with someone?   YES   NO

NOTES

_____

_____

_____

⚠ STUFF TO LOOK UP

Vocab I've learned

Goals and Deadlines

1. _____ by _____
2. _____ by _____
3. _____ by _____

Cool extras

💬 _____
💬 _____
💬 _____

(Have you worked hard enough today?)   YES   NO

YES   NO   (Are you closer to your goal today?)

Time Spent: ⏱ ⏱ ⏱ ⏱ ⏱
Motivation: 😀 🙂 😐 🙁 😣

/10

Dreams don't work unless you do
JOHN C. MAXWELL

Today's work

Active Passive

- ☑ _____ ☐ ☐
- ☑ _____ ☐ ☐
- ☑ _____ ☐ ☐
- ☑ _____ ☐ ☐

Things I have memorized

things I still can't remember

Season

Episode

Minute

!? Have you forced yourself today to speak the language with someone?   YES   NO

NOTES

_____

_____

_____

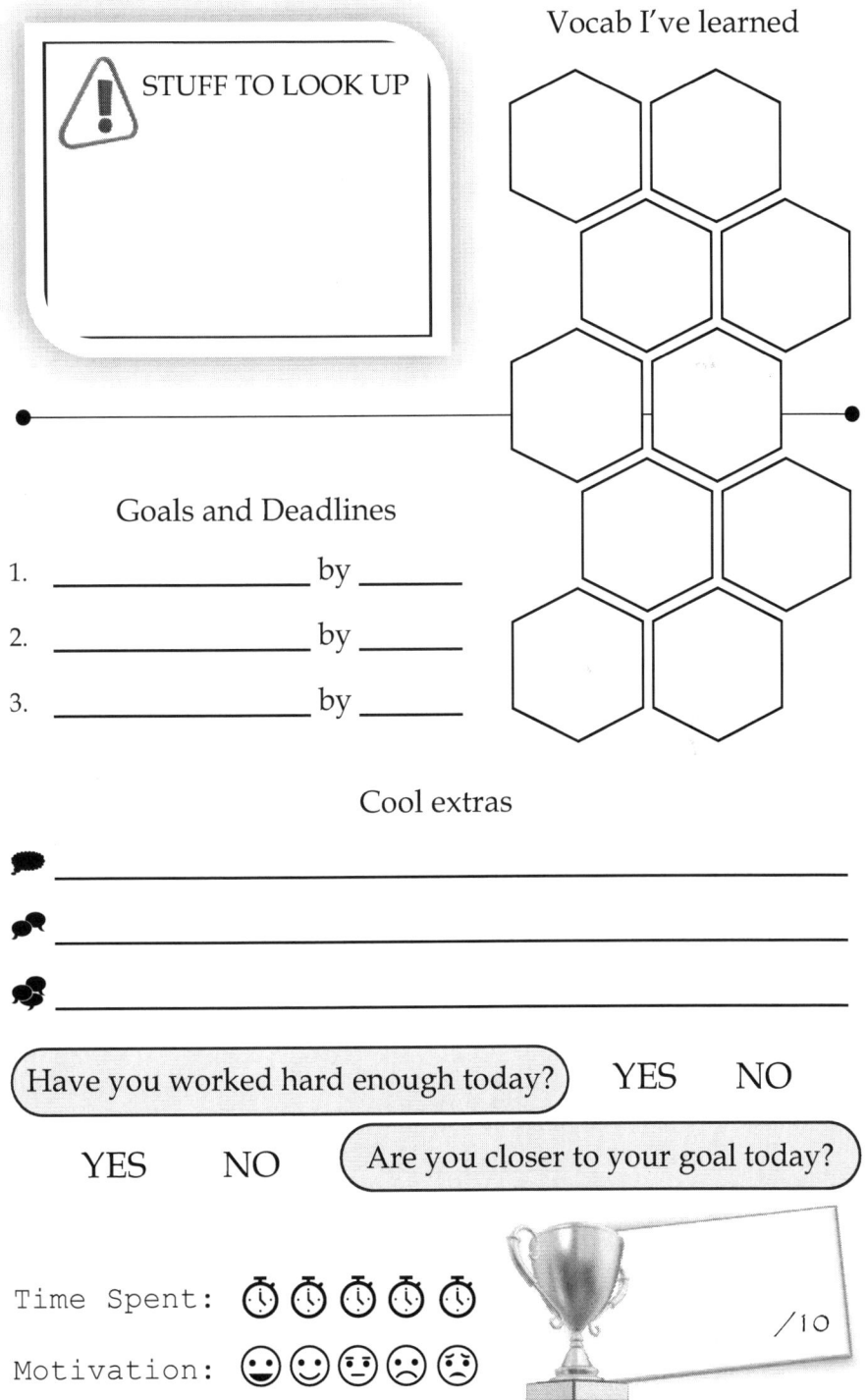

Only put off until tomorrow what you are willing to die having left undone
PABLO PICASSO

Today's work

Active Passive

- ☑ _____ ☐ ☐
- ☑ _____ ☐ ☐
- ☑ _____ ☐ ☐
- ☑ _____ ☐ ☐

Things I have memorized

things I still can't remember

Season

Episode

Minute

⁉ Have you forced yourself today to speak the language with someone?   YES   NO

NOTES

_____
_____
_____

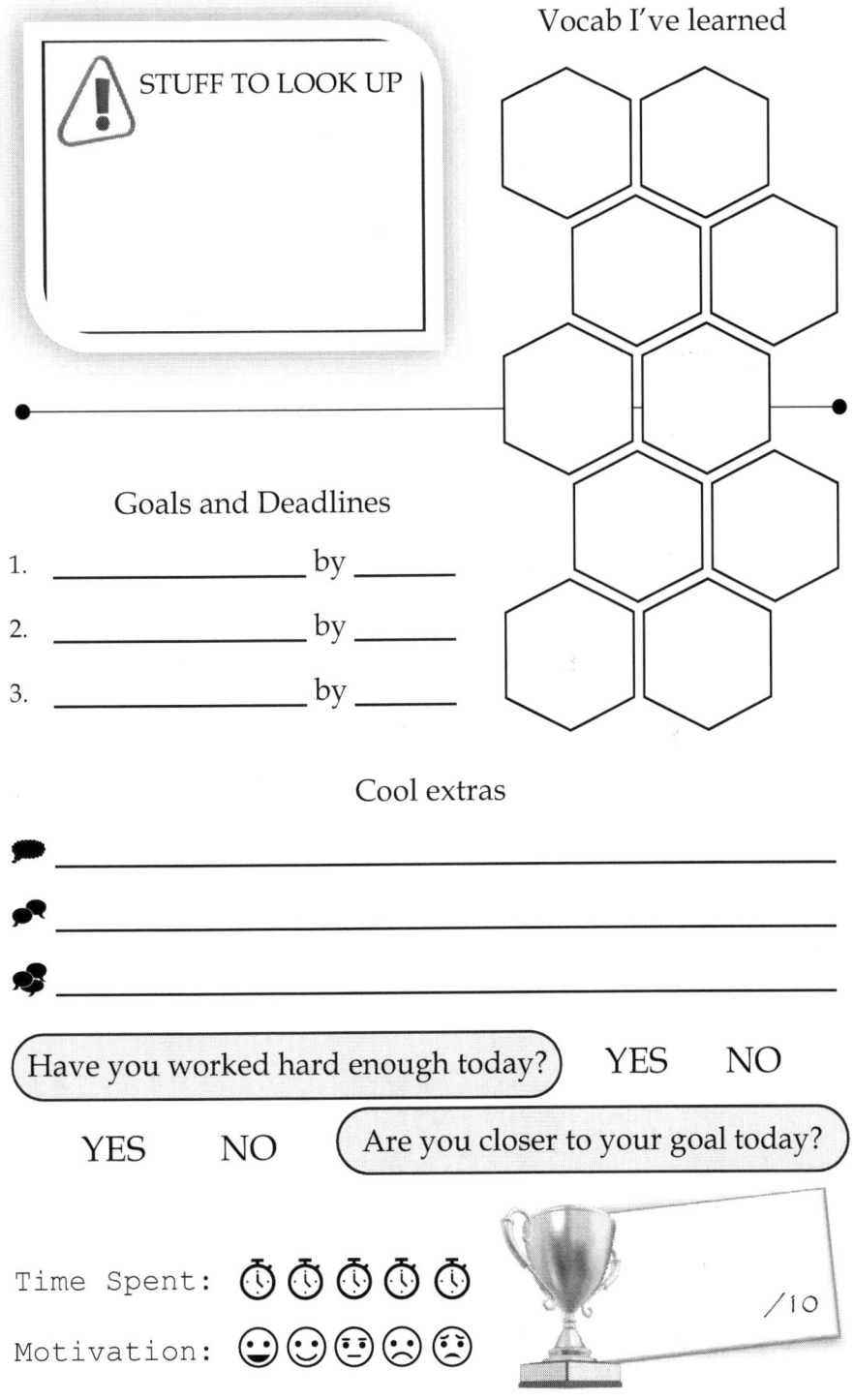

[84]

📅 ☐   ☐ 🌿

We become what we think about most of the time
EARL NIGHTINGALE

Today's work

                                                                                            Active Passive

- ☑ _____ ☐ ☐
- ☑ _____ ☐ ☐
- ☑ _____ ☐ ☐
- ☑ _____ ☐ ☐

↑ Things I have memorized

- •   •
- •   •
- •   •

↓ things I still can't remember

Season

Episode

Minute

⁉ Have you forced yourself today to speak the language with someone?   YES   NO

NOTES

_____

_____

_____

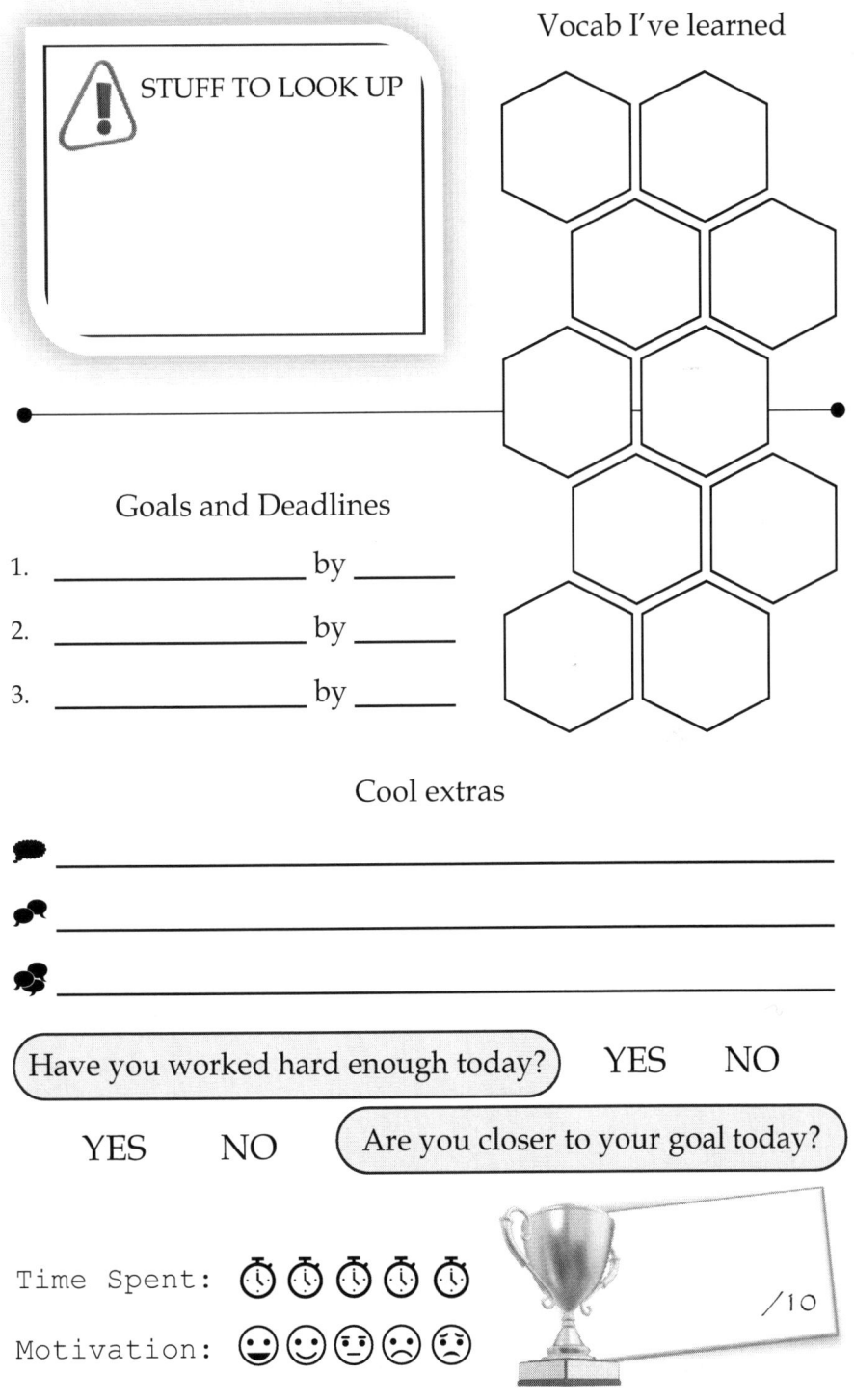

The only place where success comes before work is in the dictionary
VIDAL SASSOON

Today's work

Active   Passive

☑ _____   ☐ ☐
☑ _____   ☐ ☐
☑ _____   ☐ ☐
☑ _____   ☐ ☐

Things I have memorized

things I still can't remember

Season
Episode
Minute

⁉ Have you forced yourself today to speak the language with someone?   YES   NO

NOTES

_____
_____
_____

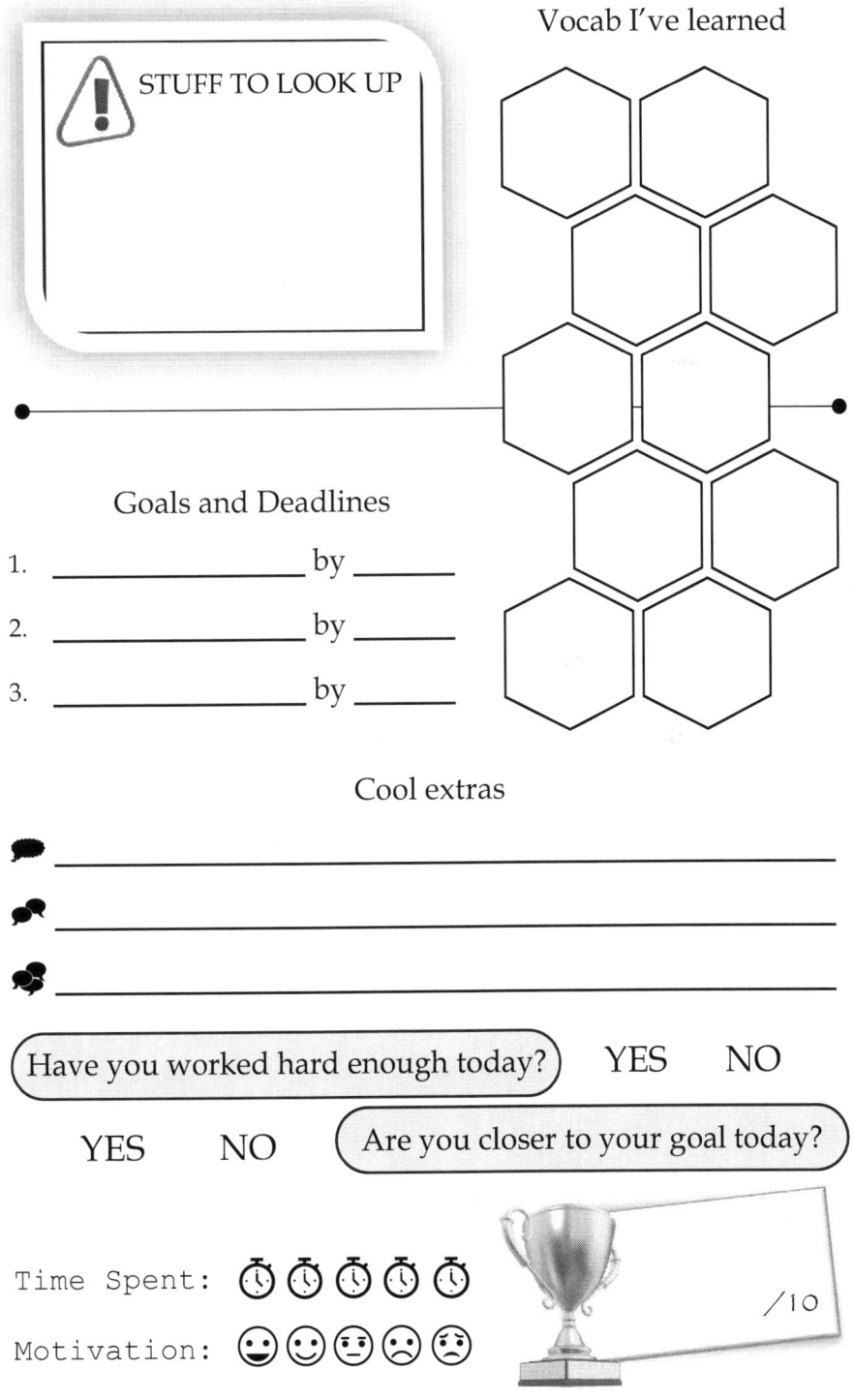

The key is in not spending time, but in investing it
STEPHEN R. COVEY

Today's work

Active Passive

- ☑ _____ ☐ ☐
- ☑ _____ ☐ ☐
- ☑ _____ ☐ ☐
- ☑ _____ ☐ ☐

Things I have memorized

things I still can't remember

Season

Episode

Minute

!? Have you forced yourself today to speak the language with someone?   YES   NO

NOTES

_____
_____
_____

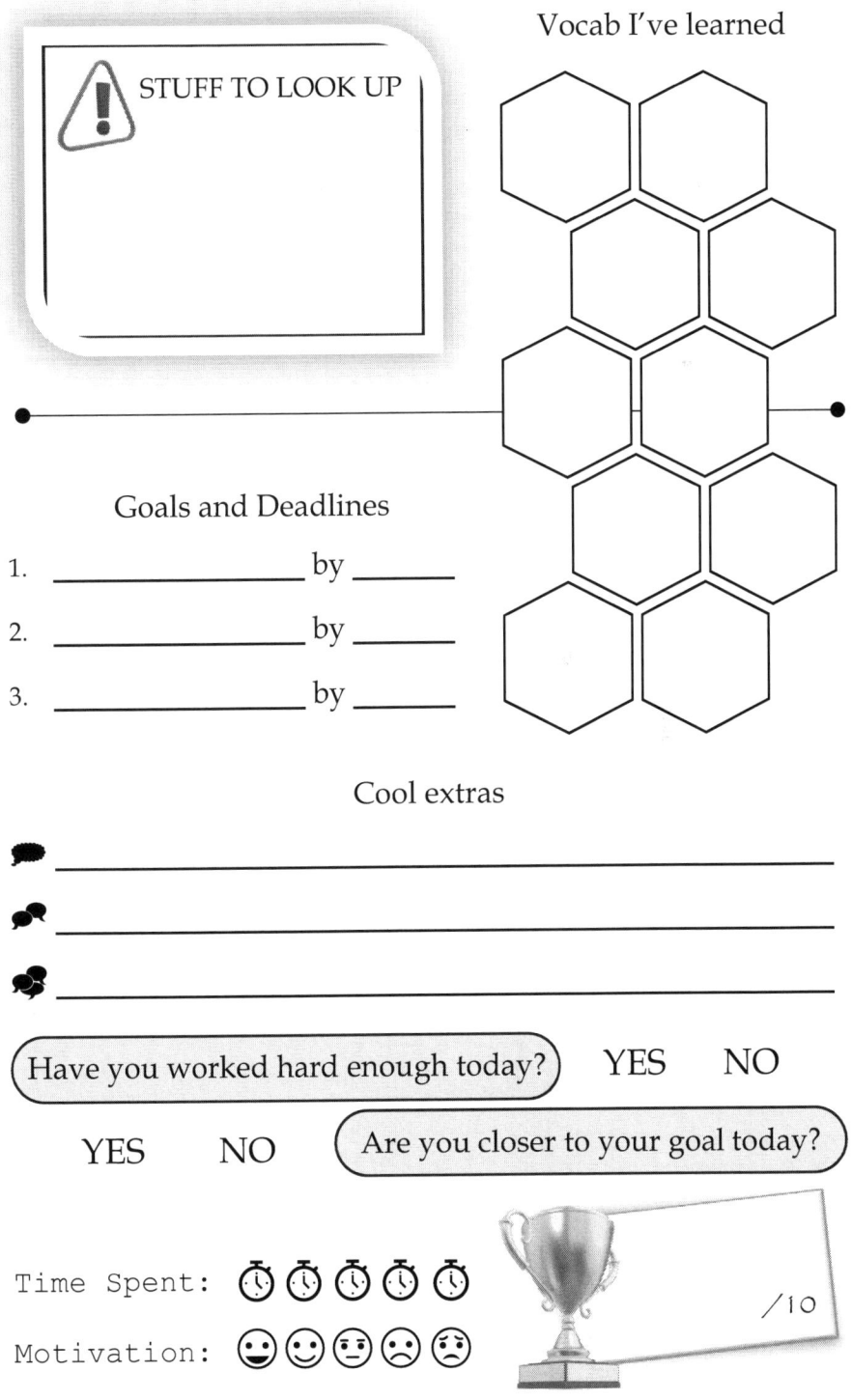

Work every day just a 1% and you'll get a 365% at the end of the year
ANONYMOUS

Today's work

Active Passive

- ☑ _____ ☐ ☐
- ☑ _____ ☐ ☐
- ☑ _____ ☐ ☐
- ☑ _____ ☐ ☐

Things I have memorized

things I still can't remember

Season

Episode

Minute

⁉ Have you forced yourself today to speak the language with someone?   YES   NO

NOTES

_____

_____

_____

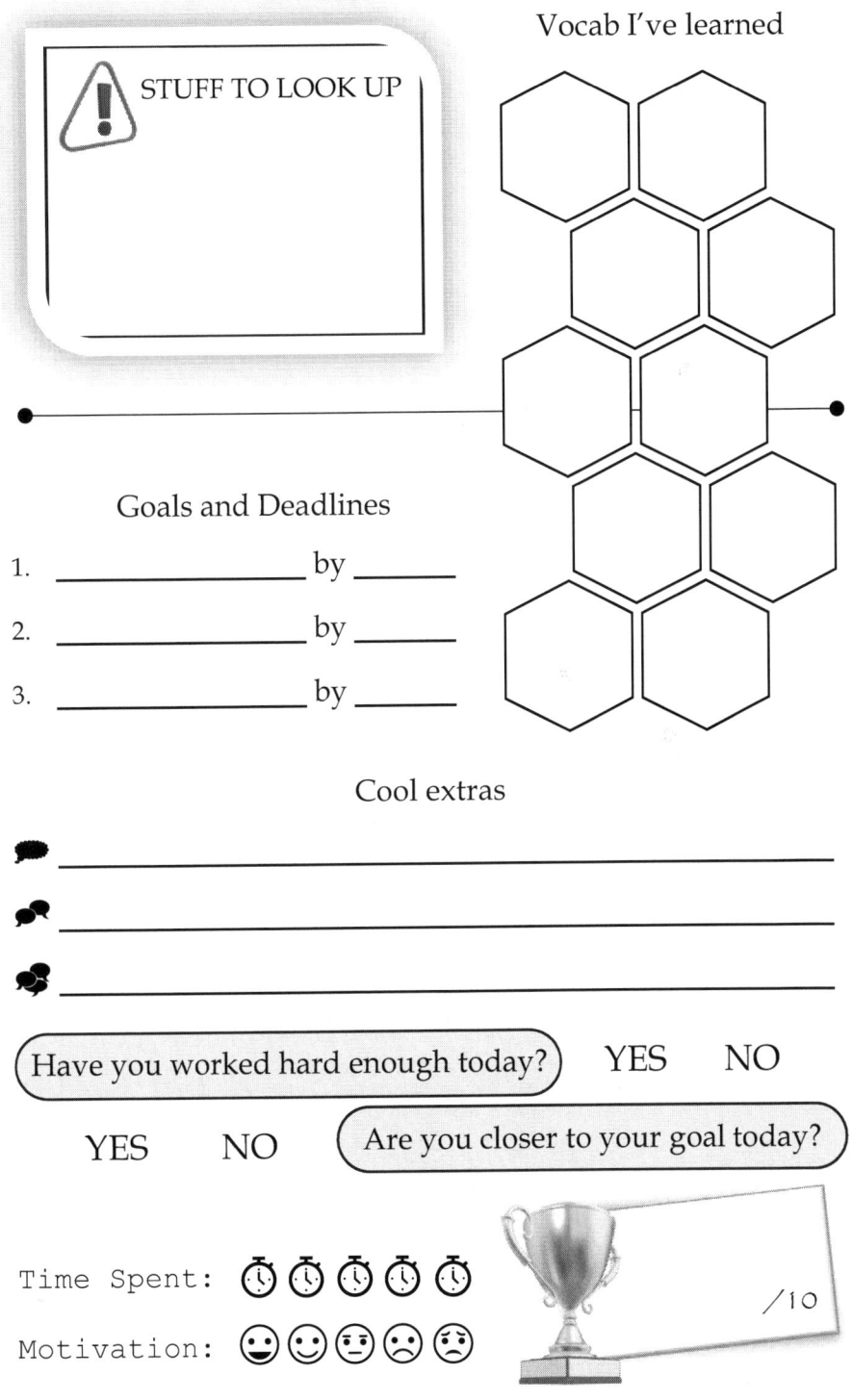

Languages will give you a better life
ROSS BY ALISTOCK

Today's work

Active Passive

☑ _____ ☐ ☐
☑ _____ ☐ ☐
☑ _____ ☐ ☐
☑ _____ ☐ ☐

Things I have memorized

things I still can't remember

Season

Episode

Minute

⁉ Have you forced yourself today to speak the language with someone?   YES   NO

NOTES

_____
_____
_____

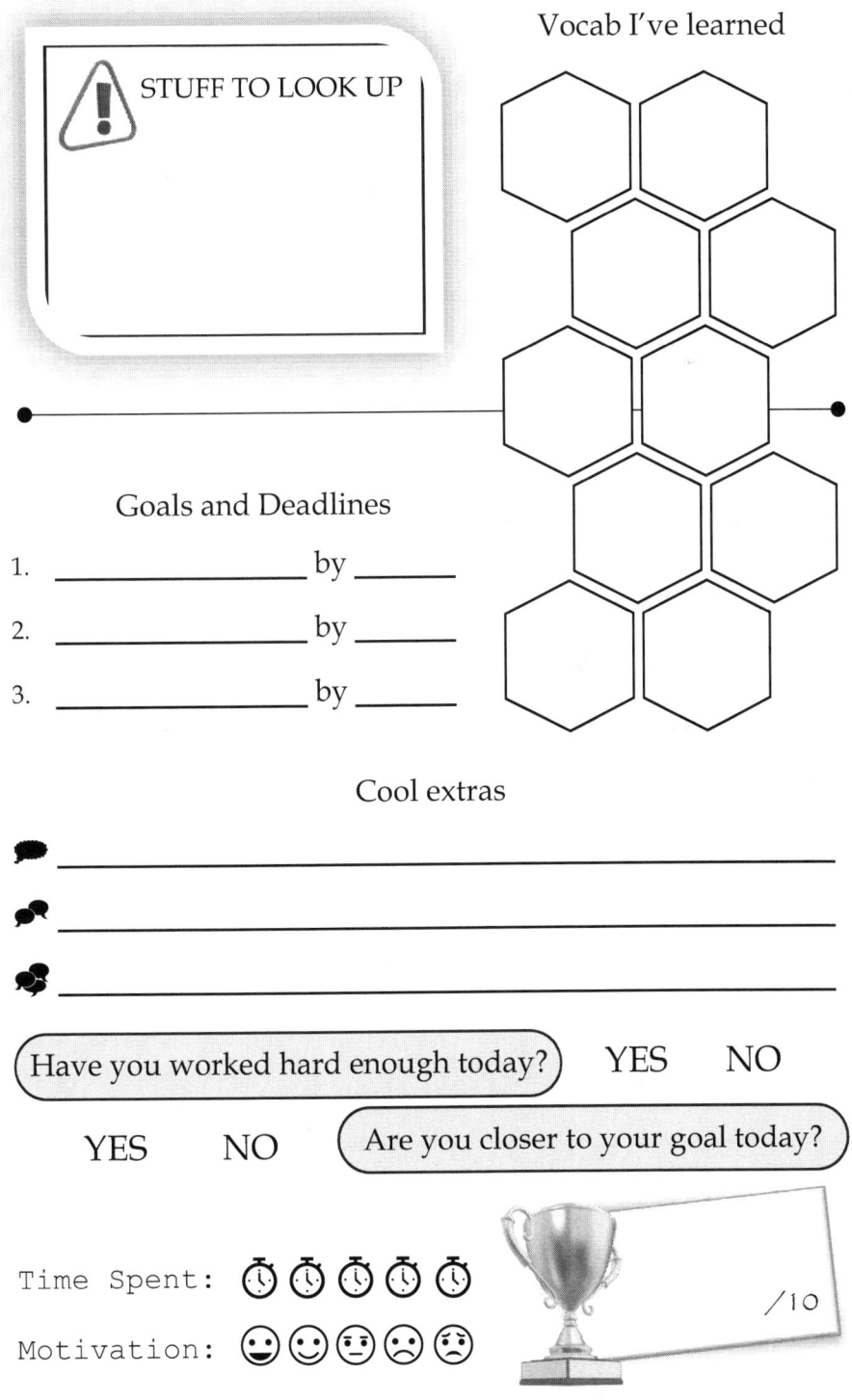

⚠ STUFF TO LOOK UP

Vocab I've learned

Goals and Deadlines

1. _____ by _____
2. _____ by _____
3. _____ by _____

Cool extras

🗨 _____
🗨 _____
🗨 _____

(Have you worked hard enough today?)   YES   NO

YES   NO   (Are you closer to your goal today?)

Time Spent: ⏱ ⏱ ⏱ ⏱ ⏱

Motivation: 😃 🙂 😐 🙁 😣

___/10

What a feeling traveling and speaking the regional language
MUIO CHIAN

Today's work

Active   Passive

- ☑ _____ ☐ ☐
- ☑ _____ ☐ ☐
- ☑ _____ ☐ ☐
- ☑ _____ ☐ ☐

Things I have memorized

things I still can't remember

Season

Episode

Minute

⚠️ Have you forced yourself today to speak the language with someone?   YES   NO

NOTES

_____

_____

_____

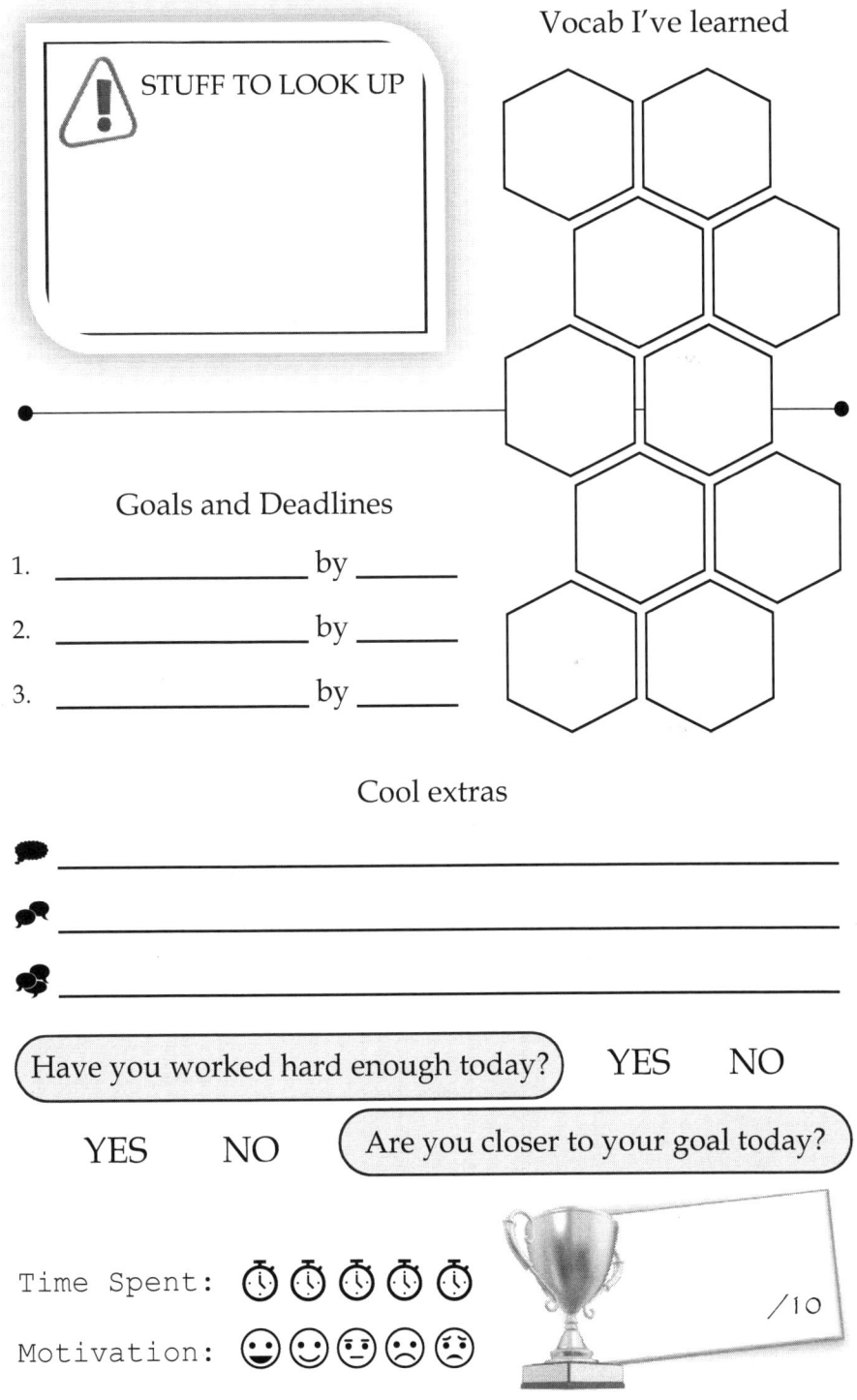

> *No polyglot can be ignorant. Languages give wisdom*
> FRAN J. WATSON

Today's work

Active Passive

- [x] _____ ☐ ☐
- [x] _____ ☐ ☐
- [x] _____ ☐ ☐
- [x] _____ ☐ ☐

Things I have memorized

things I still can't remember

Season
Episode
Minute

⁉ Have you forced yourself today to speak the language with someone?   YES   NO

NOTES

_____
_____
_____

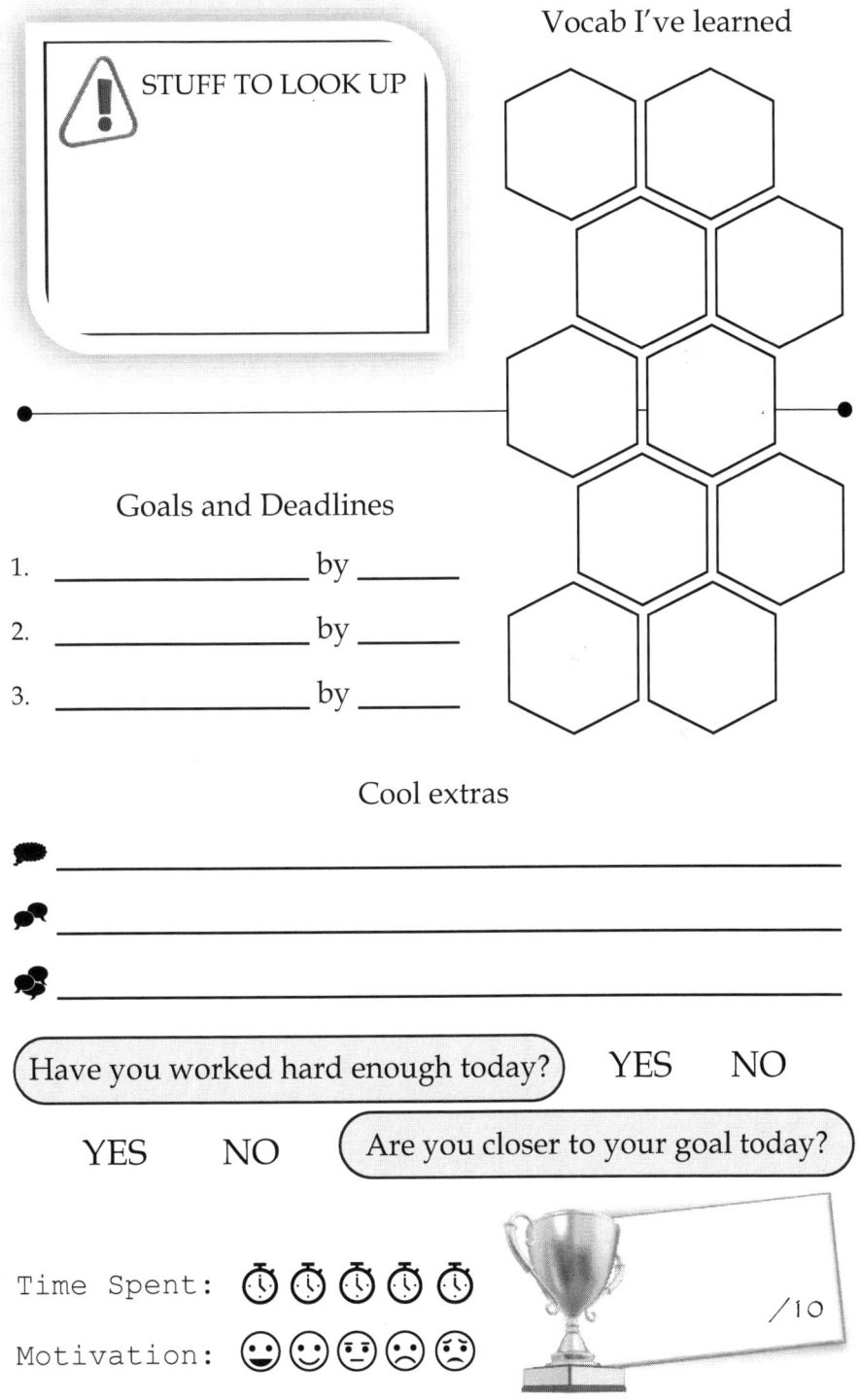

The successful warrior is the average man, with laser-like focus
BRUCE LEE

Today's work

Active Passive

- [x] _____ ☐ ☐
- [x] _____ ☐ ☐
- [x] _____ ☐ ☐
- [x] _____ ☐ ☐

Things I have memorized

things I still can't remember

Season

Episode

Minute

⚠ Have you forced yourself today to speak the language with someone?   YES   NO

NOTES

_____

_____

_____

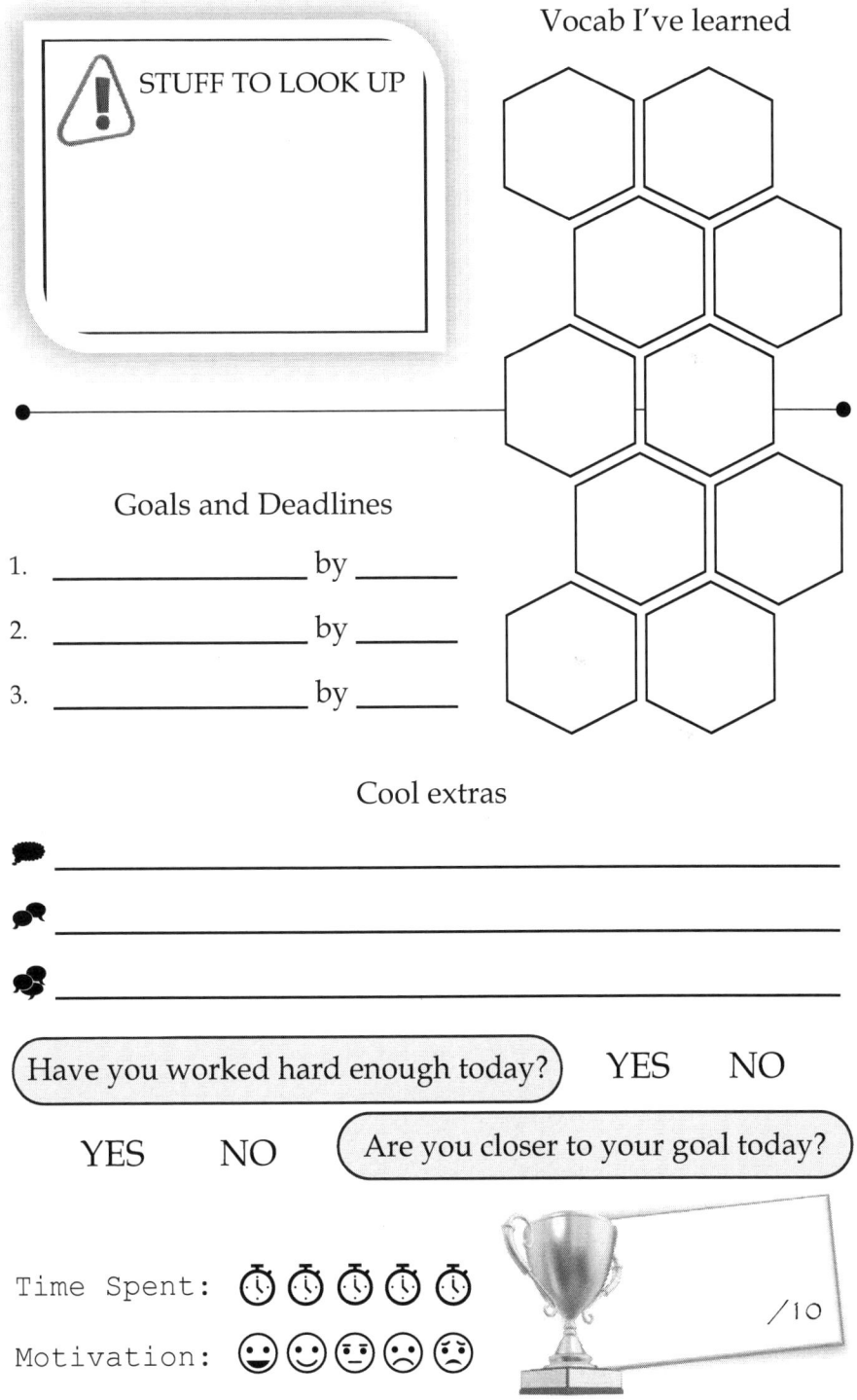

STUFF TO LOOK UP

Vocab I've learned

Goals and Deadlines

1. _____ by _____
2. _____ by _____
3. _____ by _____

Cool extras

- _____
- _____
- _____

Have you worked hard enough today?   YES   NO

YES   NO   Are you closer to your goal today?

Time Spent: 🕒 🕒 🕒 🕒 🕒

Motivation: 😀 🙂 😐 🙁 😢

/10

Don't let the fear of losing be greater than the excitement of winning
ROBERT KIYOSAKI

Today's work

Active Passive

☑ _____ ☐ ☐
☑ _____ ☐ ☐
☑ _____ ☐ ☐
☑ _____ ☐ ☐

Things I have memorized

- •   •
- •   •
- •   •

things I still can't remember

Season

Episode

Minute

⚠ Have you forced yourself today to speak the language with someone?   YES   NO

NOTES

_____
_____
_____

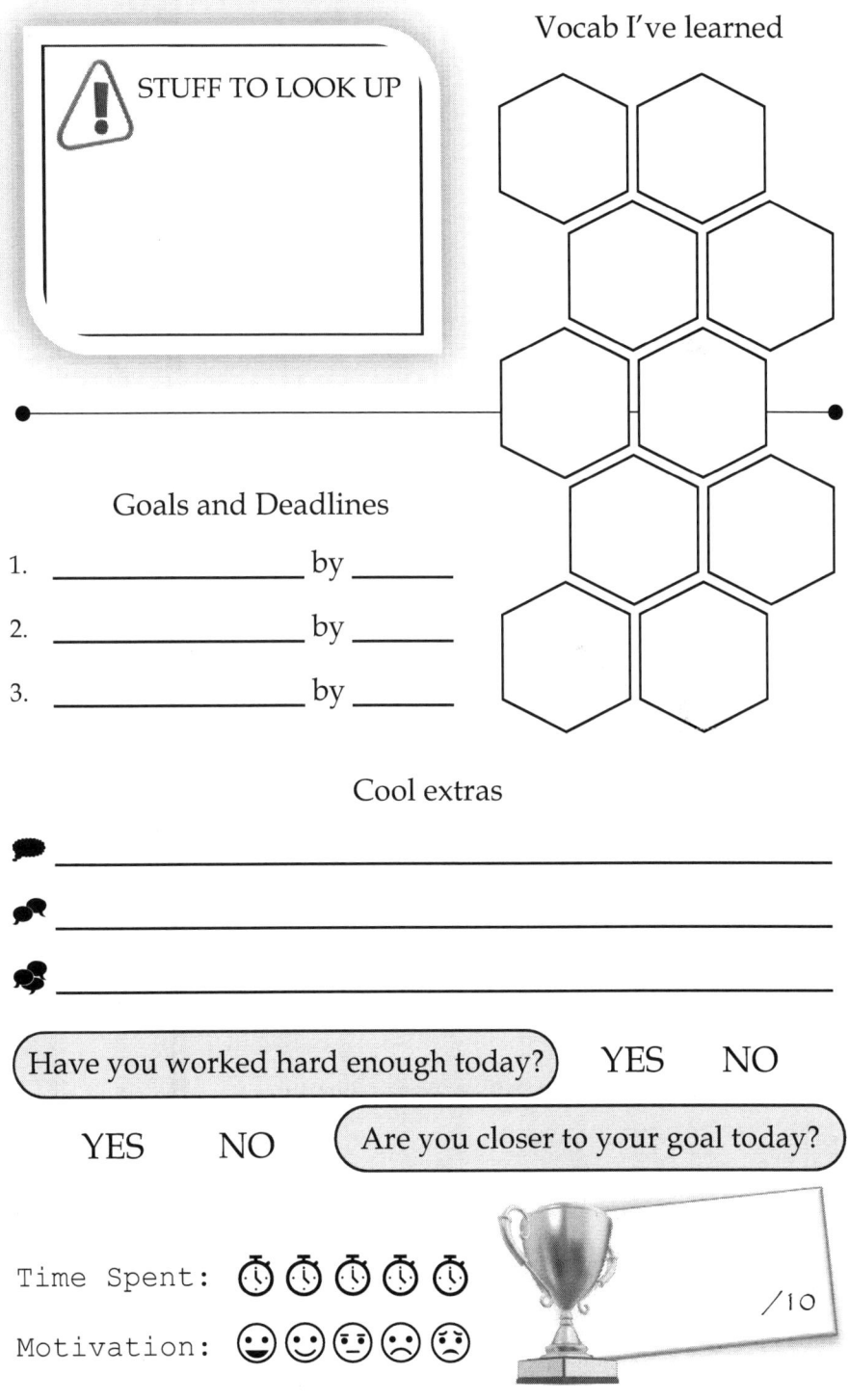

You must expect great things of yourself before you can do them
MICHAEL JORDAN

Today's work

Active Passive

- ☑ _____ ☐ ☐
- ☑ _____ ☐ ☐
- ☑ _____ ☐ ☐
- ☑ _____ ☐ ☐

Things I have memorized

things I still can't remember

Season

Episode

Minute

⁉ Have you forced yourself today to speak the language with someone?   YES   NO

NOTES

_____
_____
_____

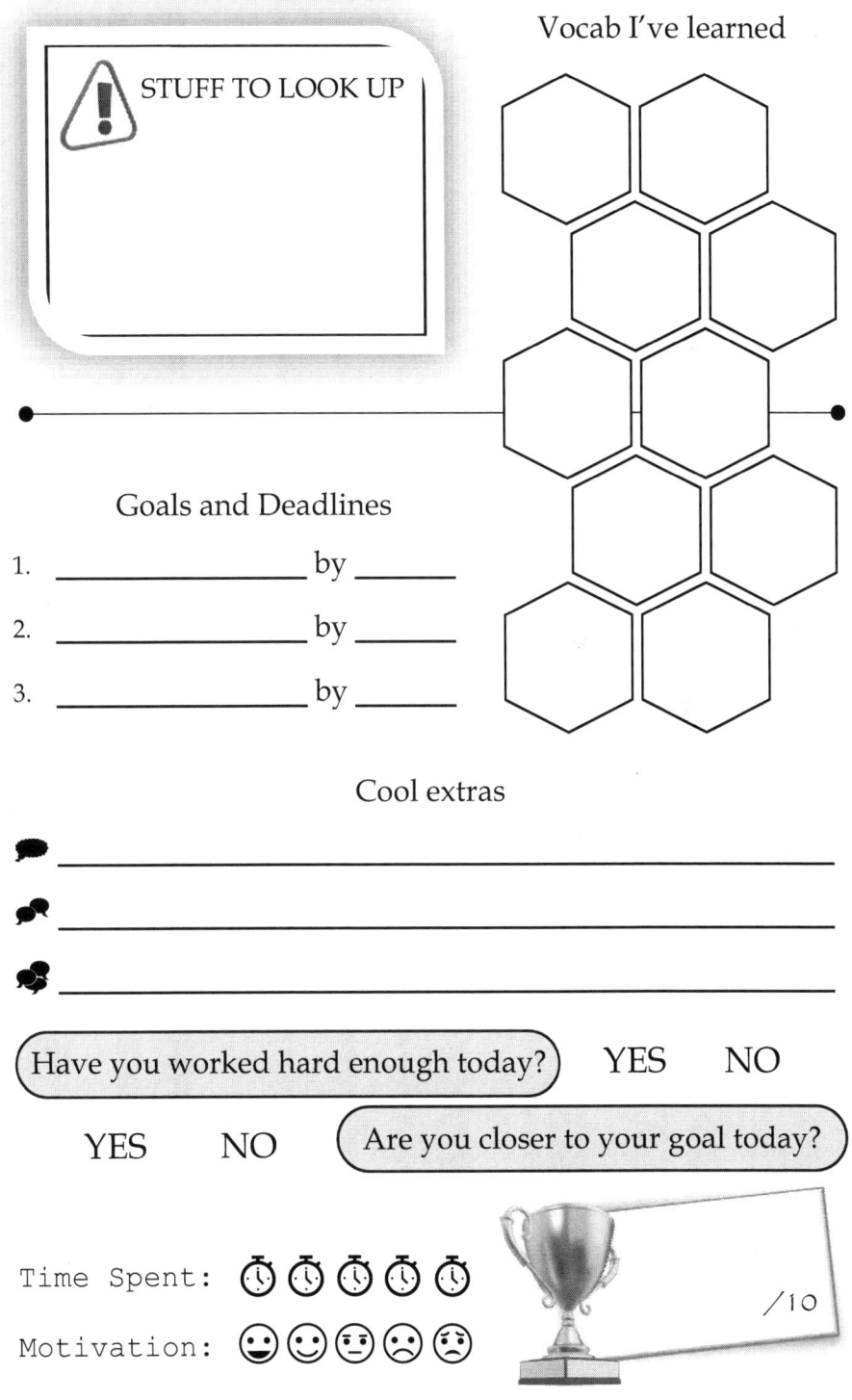

Motivation is what gets you started. Habit is what keeps you going
JIM RYAN

Today's work

Active   Passive

☑ _____ ☐ ☐
☑ _____ ☐ ☐
☑ _____ ☐ ☐
☑ _____ ☐ ☐

Things I have memorized

• •
• •
• •

things I still can't remember

Season

Episode

Minute

⁉ Have you forced yourself today to speak the language with someone?   YES   NO

NOTES

_____
_____
_____

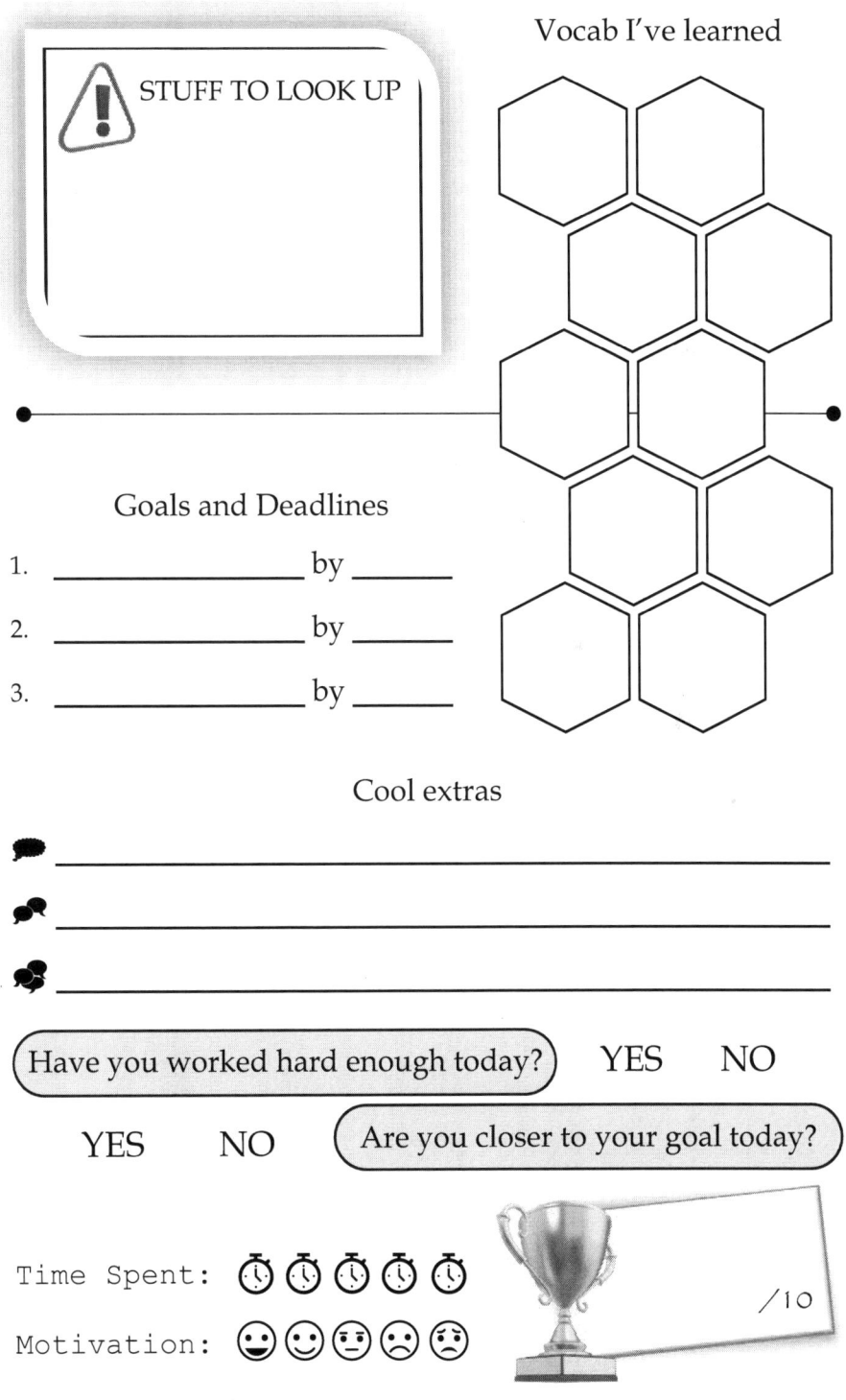

[106]

People rarely succeed unless they have fun in what they are doing
DALE CARNEGIE

Today's work

Active   Passive

☑ _____ ☐ ☐

☑ _____ ☐ ☐

☑ _____ ☐ ☐

☑ _____ ☐ ☐

Things I have memorized

• | •
• | •
• | •

things I still can't remember

Season

Episode

Minute

⁉ Have you forced yourself today to speak the language with someone?   YES   NO

NOTES

_____

_____

_____

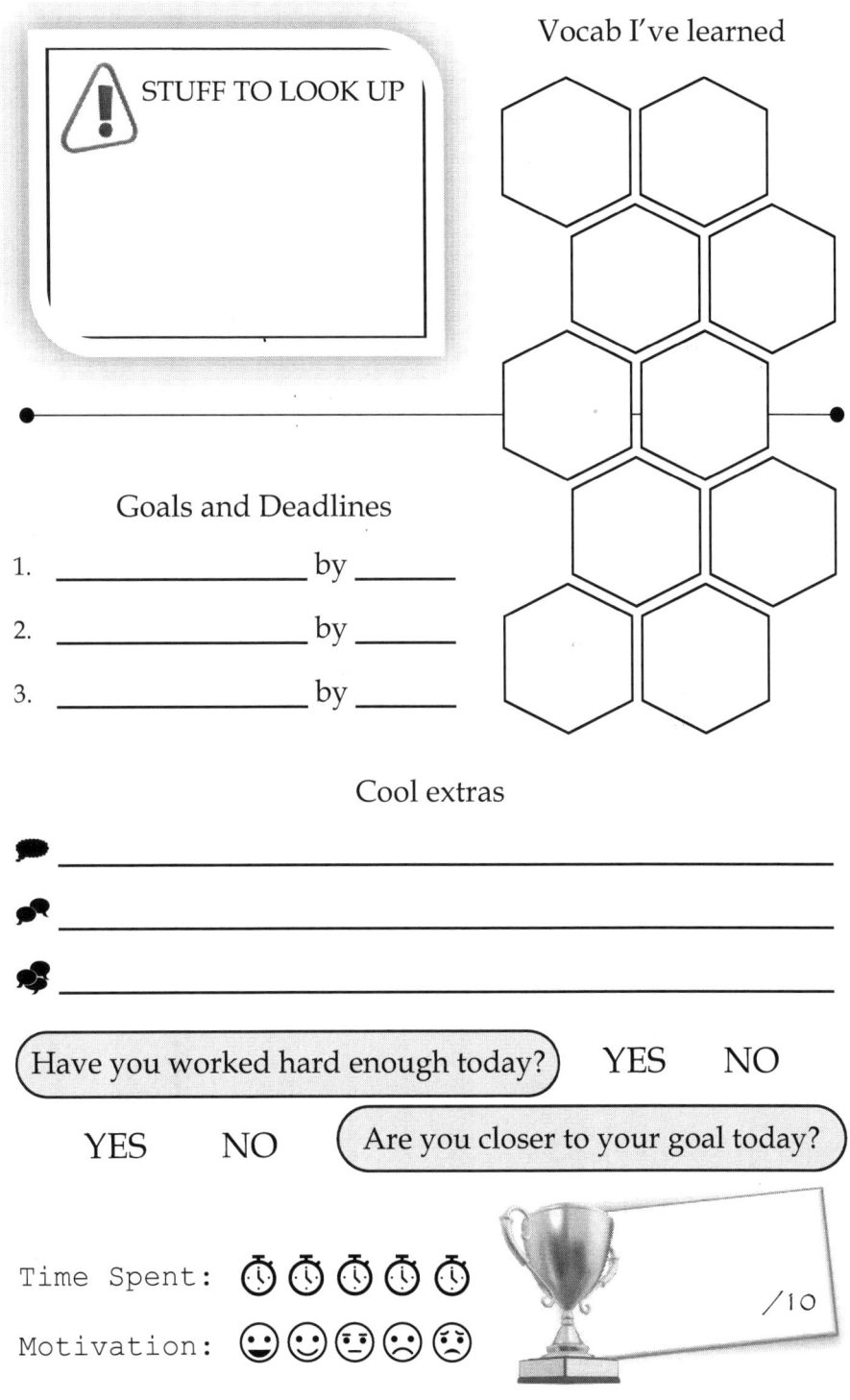

It is better to fail in originality than to succeed in imitation
HERMAN MELVILLE

Today's work

Active Passive

☑ _____ ☐ ☐
☑ _____ ☐ ☐
☑ _____ ☐ ☐
☑ _____ ☐ ☐

Things I have memorized

• •
• •
• •

things I still can't remember

Season
Episode
Minute

⁉ Have you forced yourself today to speak the language with someone?   YES   NO

NOTES

_____
_____
_____

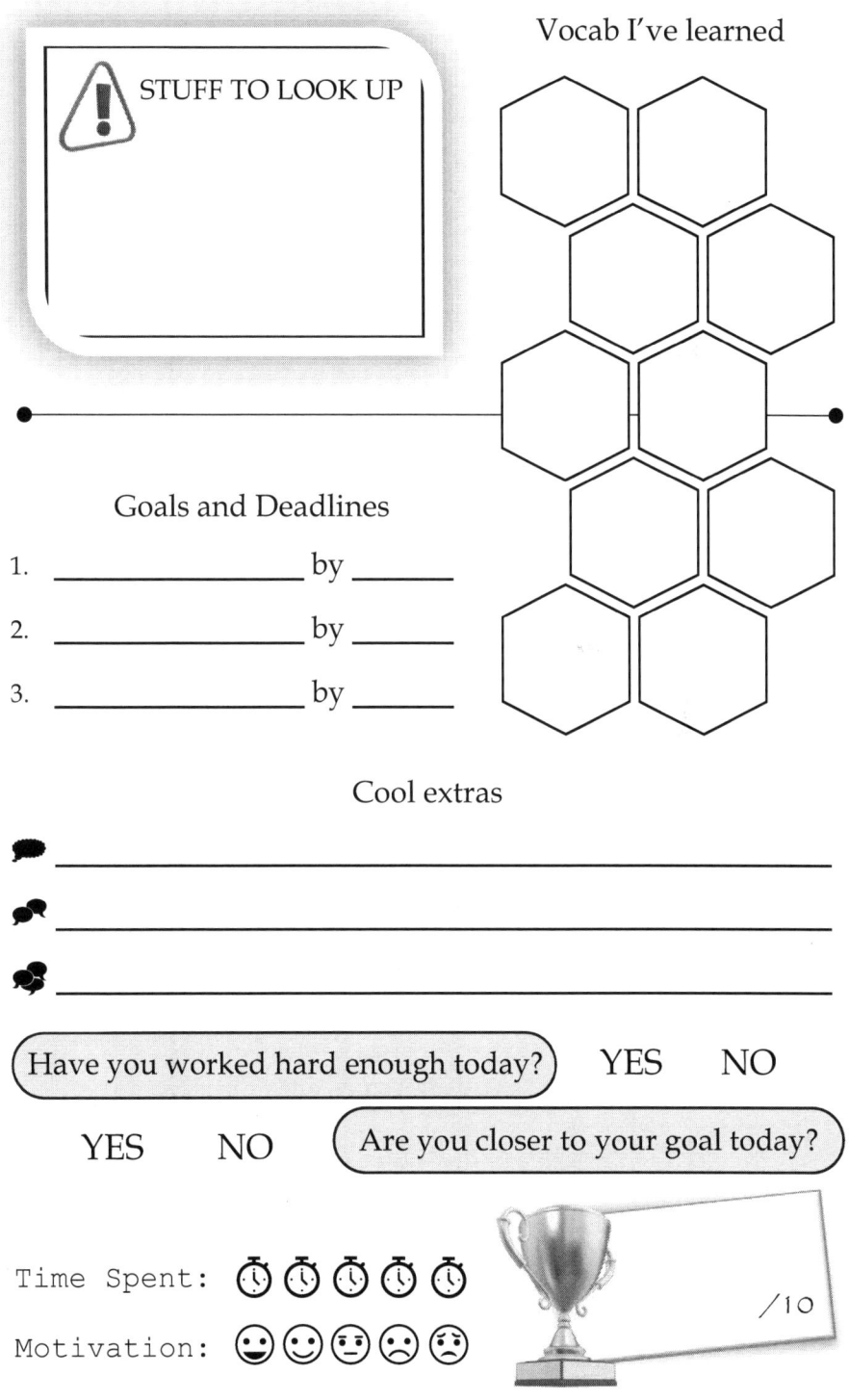

Fortune sides with him who dares
VIRGIL

Today's work

Active Passive

- [x] _____ ☐ ☐
- [x] _____ ☐ ☐
- [x] _____ ☐ ☐
- [x] _____ ☐ ☐

Things I have memorized

things I still can't remember

Season

Episode

Minute

⁉ Have you forced yourself today to speak the language with someone?   YES   NO

NOTES

_____

_____

_____

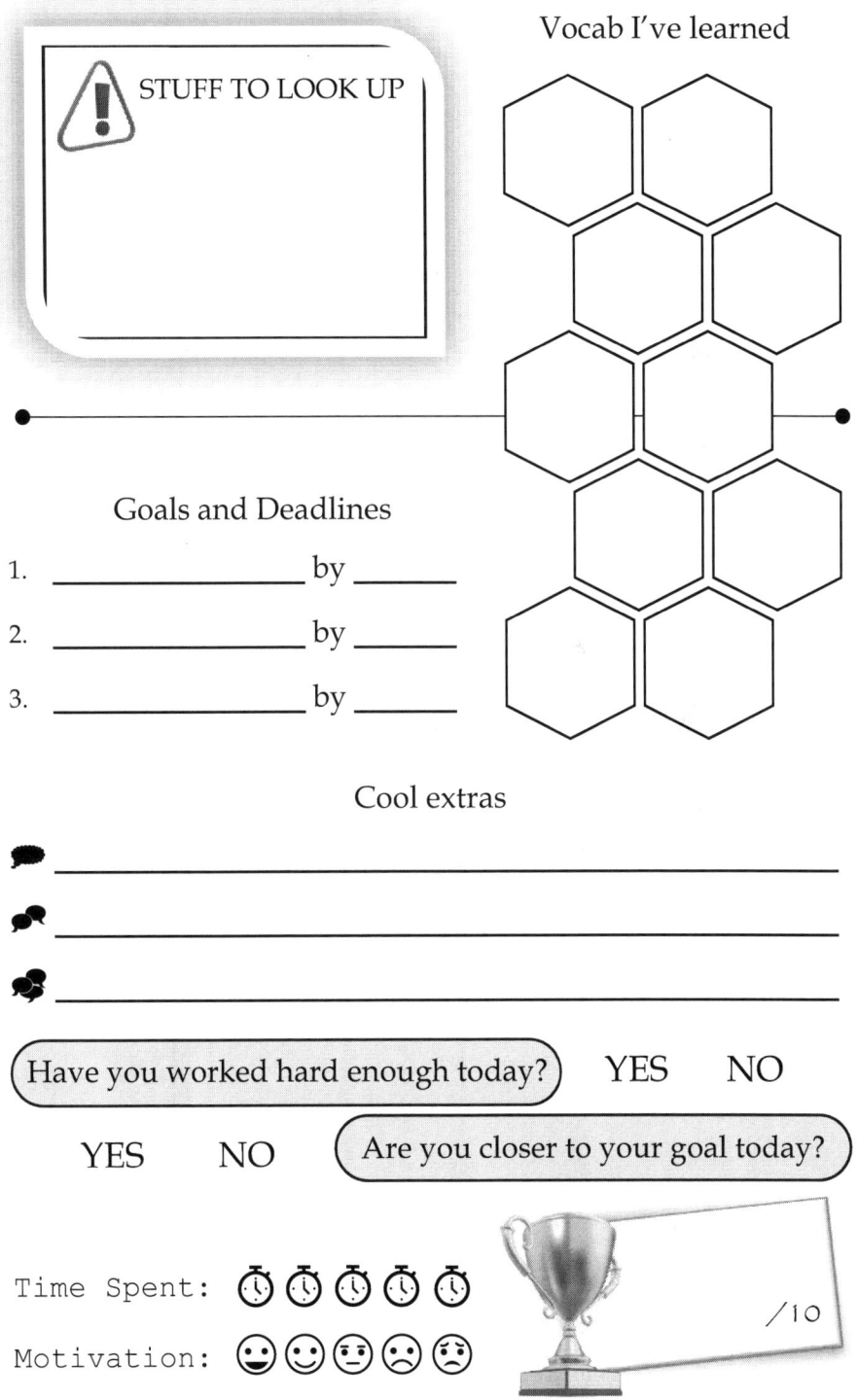

If you want to achieve greatness stop asking for permission
ANONYMOUS

Today's work

Active   Passive

☑ _____ ☐ ☐
☑ _____ ☐ ☐
☑ _____ ☐ ☐
☑ _____ ☐ ☐

Things I have memorized

things I still can't remember

Season

Episode

Minute

⁉ Have you forced yourself today to speak the language with someone?   YES   NO

NOTES

_____
_____
_____

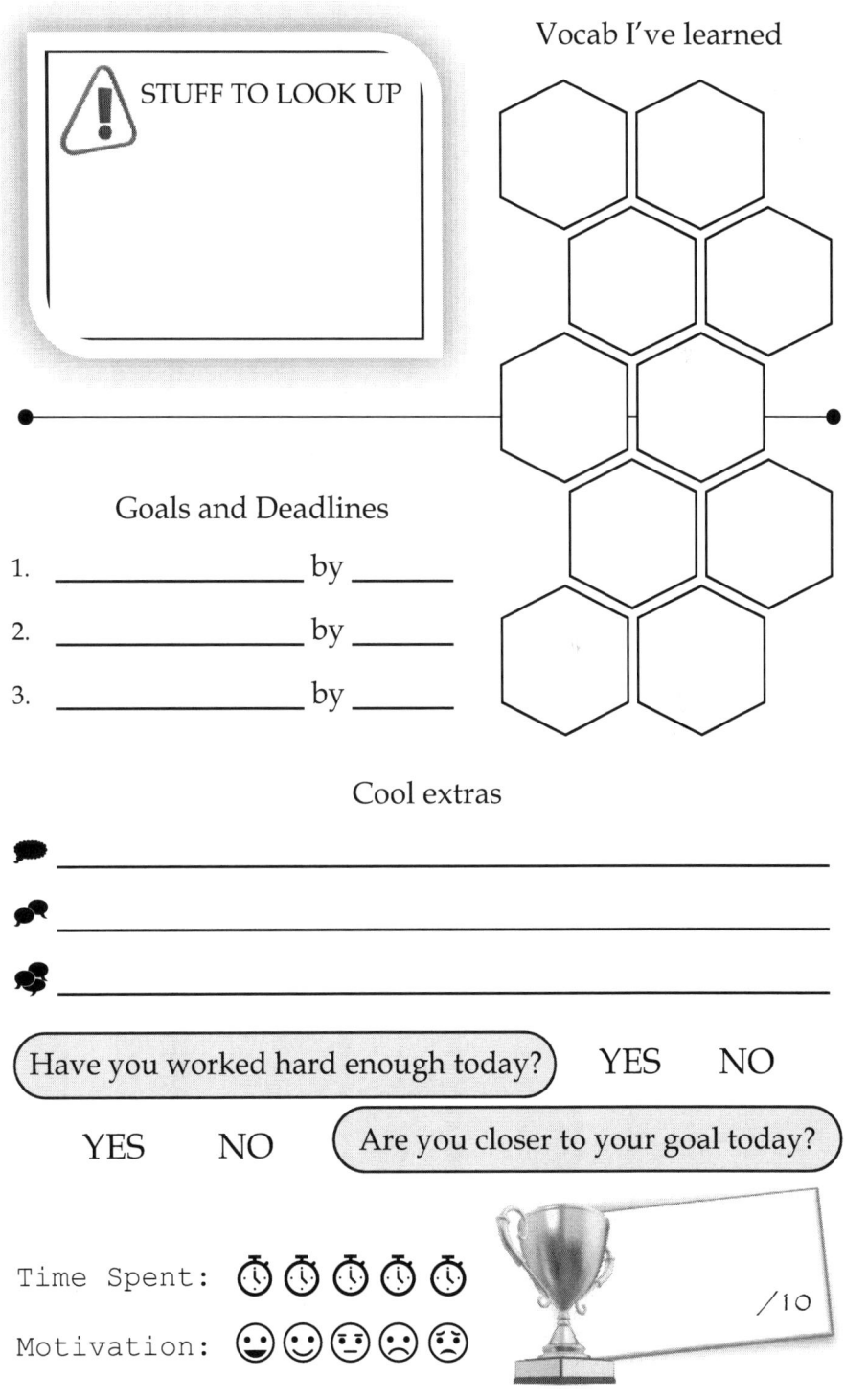

Things work out best for those who make the best of how things work out
JOHN WOODEN

Today's work

Active Passive

☑ _____ ☐ ☐
☑ _____ ☐ ☐
☑ _____ ☐ ☐
☑ _____ ☐ ☐

Things I have memorized

things I still can't remember

Season

Episode

Minute

⁉ Have you forced yourself today to speak the language with someone?   YES   NO

NOTES

_____
_____
_____

⚠ STUFF TO LOOK UP

Vocab I've learned

Goals and Deadlines

1. _____ by _____
2. _____ by _____
3. _____ by _____

Cool extras

💬 _____
💬 _____
💬 _____

(Have you worked hard enough today?)   YES   NO

YES   NO   (Are you closer to your goal today?)

Time Spent: ⏱ ⏱ ⏱ ⏱ ⏱

Motivation: 😃 🙂 😐 🙁 😣

/10

To live a creative life, we must lose our fear of being wrong
ANONYMOUS

Today's work

Active Passive

- ☑ _____ ☐ ☐
- ☑ _____ ☐ ☐
- ☑ _____ ☐ ☐
- ☑ _____ ☐ ☐

Things I have memorized

things I still can't remember

Season

Episode

Minute

⁉ Have you forced yourself today to speak the language with someone?   YES   NO

NOTES

_____
_____
_____

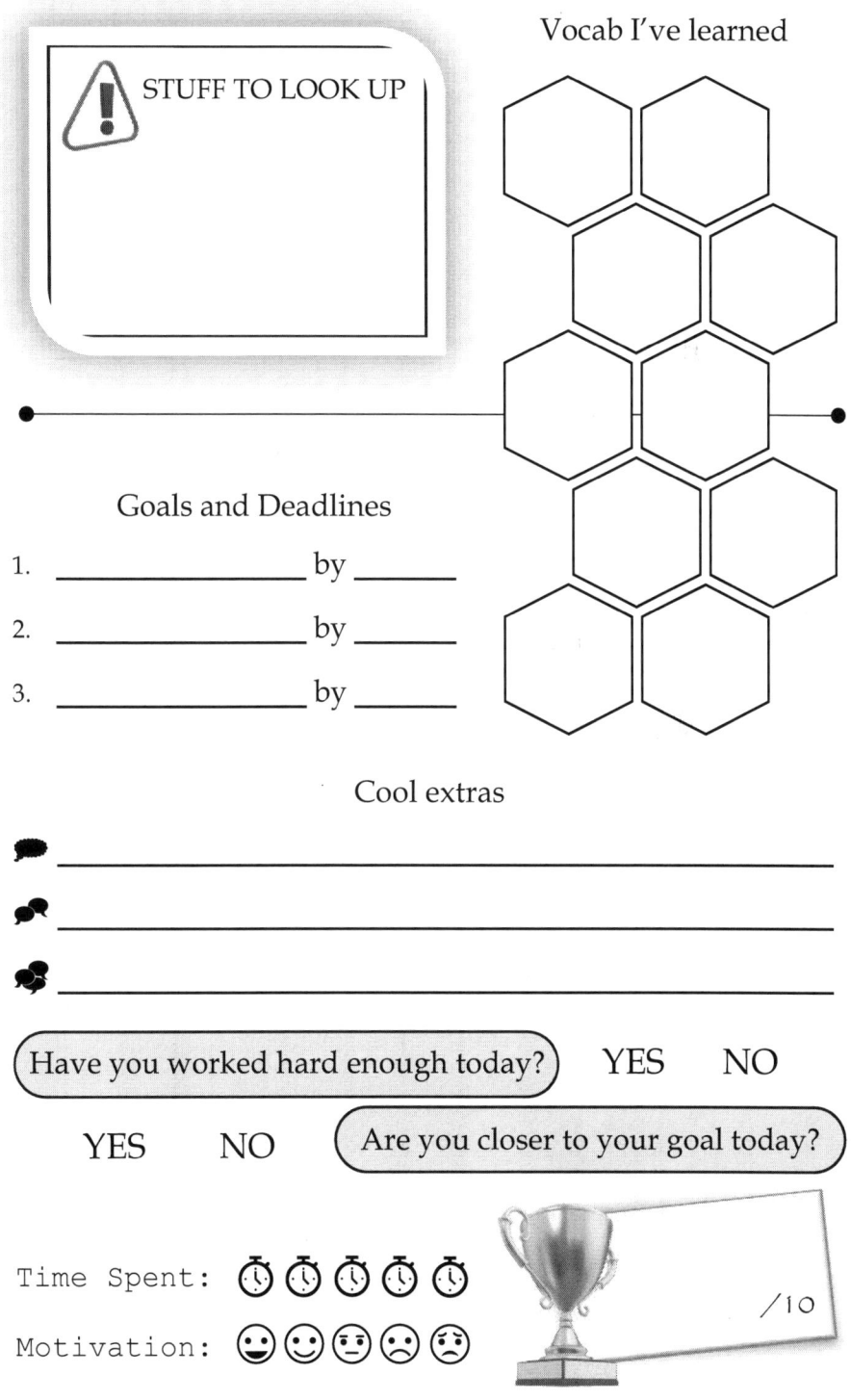

If you are not willing to risk the usual you will have to settle for the ordinary
JIM ROHN

Today's work   Active   Passive

☑ _____   ☐   ☐
☑ _____   ☐   ☐
☑ _____   ☐   ☐
☑ _____   ☐   ☐

Things I have memorized

• •
• •
• •

things I still can't remember

Season

Episode

Minute

⁉ Have you forced yourself today to speak the language with someone?   YES   NO

NOTES

_____
_____
_____

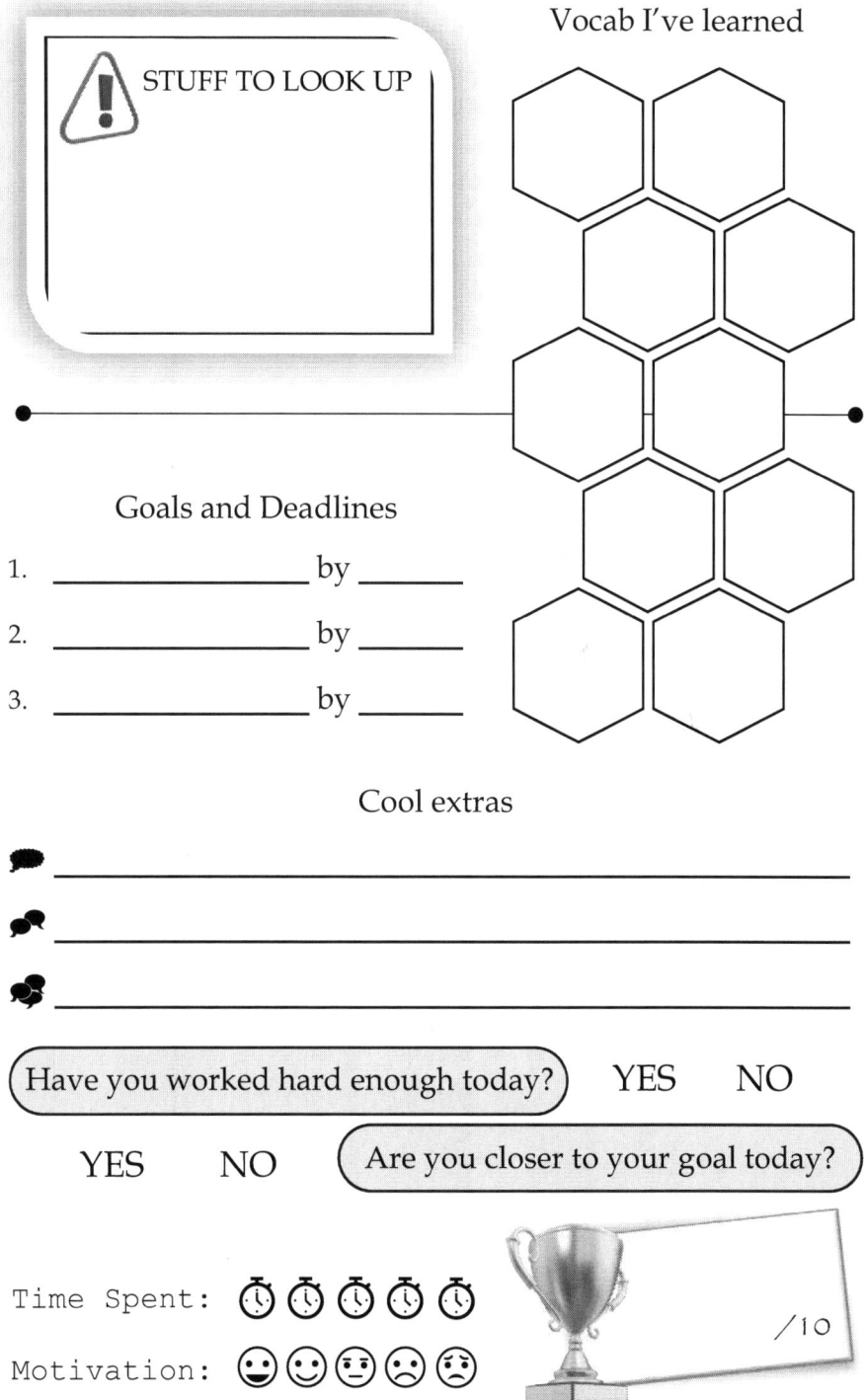

⚠ STUFF TO LOOK UP

Vocab I've learned

Goals and Deadlines

1. _____ by _____
2. _____ by _____
3. _____ by _____

Cool extras

🗨 _____
🗨 _____
🗨 _____

(Have you worked hard enough today?)   YES   NO

YES   NO   (Are you closer to your goal today?)

Time Spent: ⏱ ⏱ ⏱ ⏱ ⏱

Motivation: 😀 🙂 😐 🙁 😣

/10

Trust because you are willing to accept the risk, not because it's safe or certain
ANONYMOUS

Today's work

Active Passive

☑ _____ ☐ ☐
☑ _____ ☐ ☐
☑ _____ ☐ ☐
☑ _____ ☐ ☐

Things I have memorized

- •   •
- •   •
- •   •

things I still can't remember

Season

Episode

Minute

⁉ Have you forced yourself today to speak the language with someone?   YES   NO

NOTES

_____

_____

_____

⚠ STUFF TO LOOK UP

Vocab I've learned

Goals and Deadlines

1. _____ by _____
2. _____ by _____
3. _____ by _____

Cool extras

💬 _____
💬 _____
💬 _____

(Have you worked hard enough today?)   YES   NO

YES   NO   (Are you closer to your goal today?)

Time Spent: 🕐 🕐 🕐 🕐 🕐
Motivation: 😀 🙂 😐 🙁 😟

/10

All our dreams can come true if we have the courage to pursue them
WALT DISNEY

Today's work

Active Passive

☑ _____ ☐ ☐
☑ _____ ☐ ☐
☑ _____ ☐ ☐
☑ _____ ☐ ☐

Things I have memorized
-
-
-

things I still can't remember

Season

Episode

Minute

⁉ Have you forced yourself today to speak the language with someone?   YES   NO

NOTES

_____
_____
_____

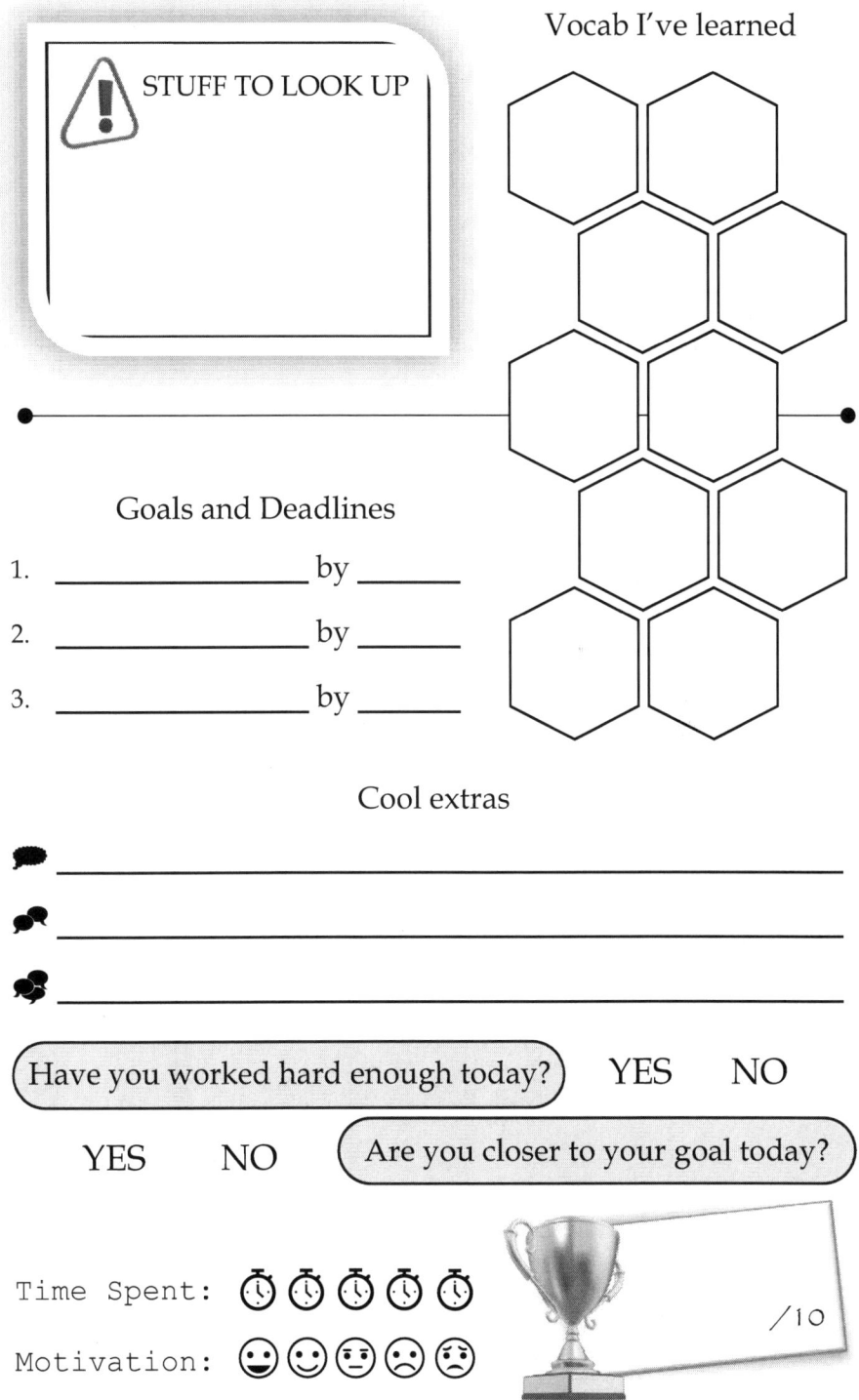

If you do what you always did, you will get what you always got
ANONYMOUS

Today's work

Active Passive

☑ _____ ☐ ☐
☑ _____ ☐ ☐
☑ _____ ☐ ☐
☑ _____ ☐ ☐

Things I have memorized

• •
• •
• •

things I still can't remember

Season

Episode

Minute

⁉ Have you forced yourself today to speak the language with someone?   YES   NO

NOTES

_____
_____
_____

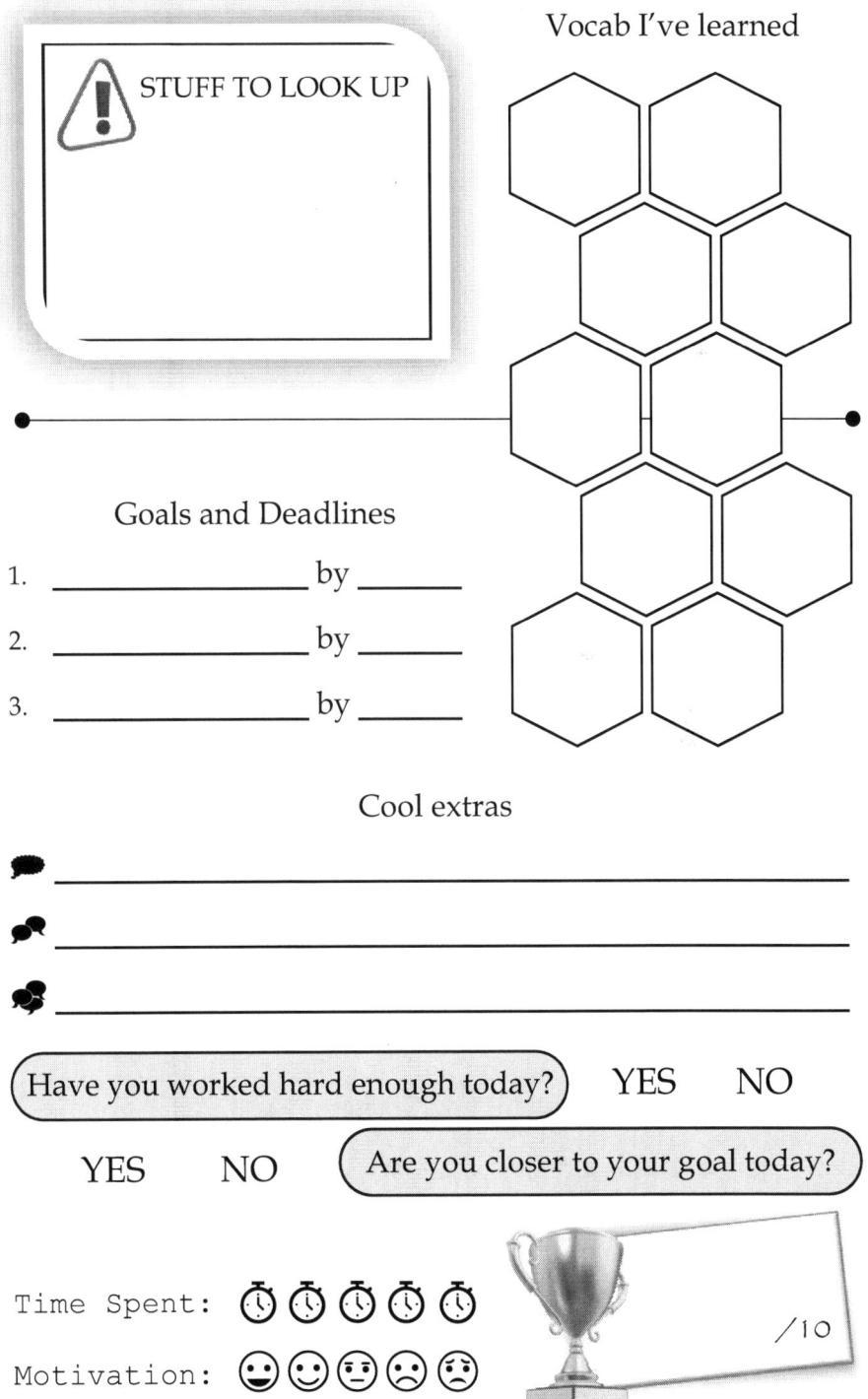

STUFF TO LOOK UP

Vocab I've learned

Goals and Deadlines

1. _____ by ____
2. _____ by ____
3. _____ by ____

Cool extras

- _____
- _____
- _____

Have you worked hard enough today?   YES   NO

YES   NO   Are you closer to your goal today?

Time Spent:
Motivation:

/10

Success is walking from failure to failure with no loss of enthusiasm
WINSTON CHURCHILL

Today's work

Active Passive

☑ _____ ☐ ☐
☑ _____ ☐ ☐
☑ _____ ☐ ☐
☑ _____ ☐ ☐

Things I have memorized

things I still can't remember

Season
Episode
Minute

⁉ Have you forced yourself today to speak the language with someone?   YES   NO

NOTES

_____
_____
_____

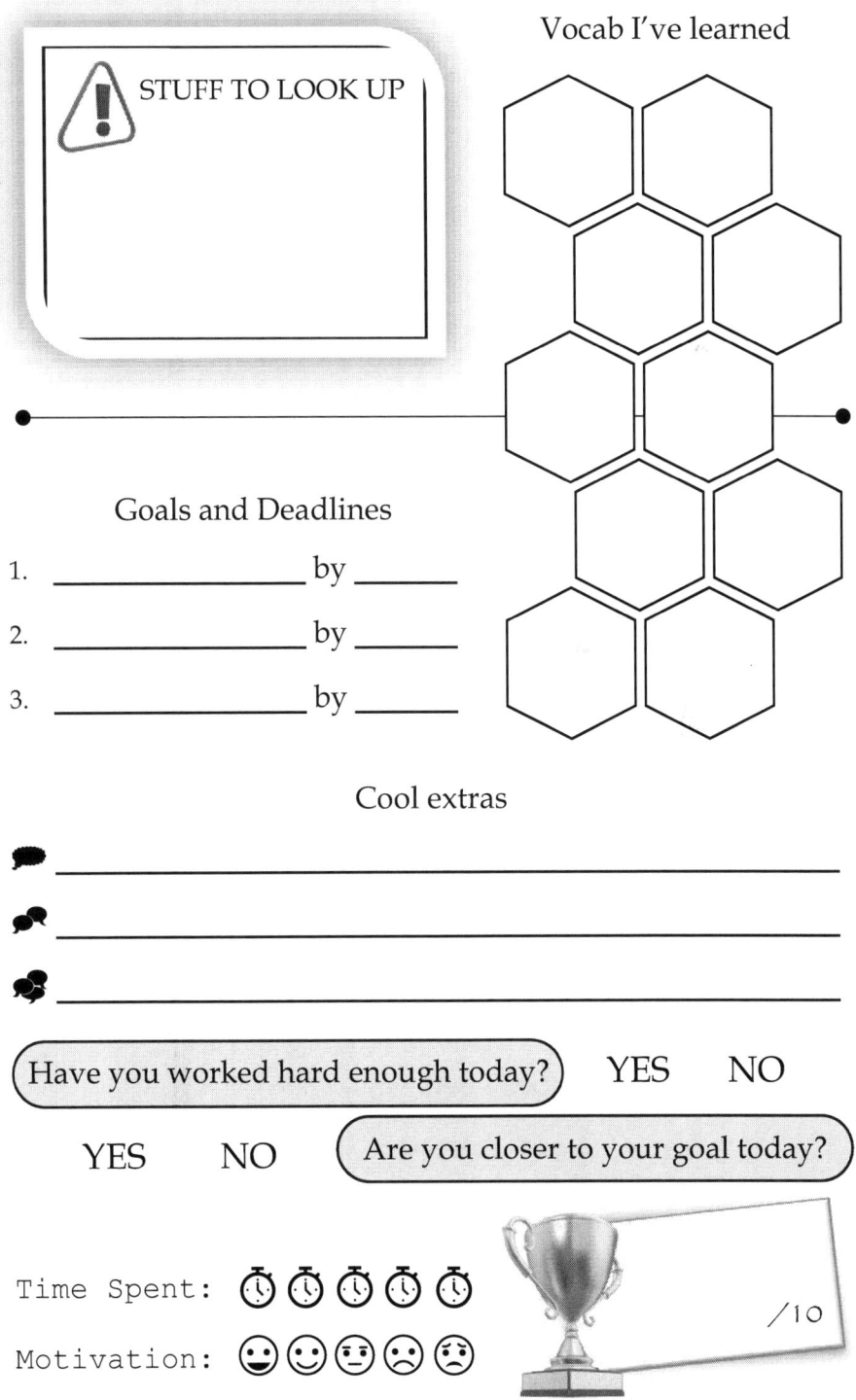

Just when the caterpillar thought the world was ending, he turned into a butterfly
CHINESE PROVERB

Today's work

Active Passive

☑ _____ ☐ ☐
☑ _____ ☐ ☐
☑ _____ ☐ ☐
☑ _____ ☐ ☐

Things I have memorized

things I still can't remember

Season

Episode

Minute

⁉ Have you forced yourself today to speak the language with someone?   YES   NO

NOTES

_____
_____
_____

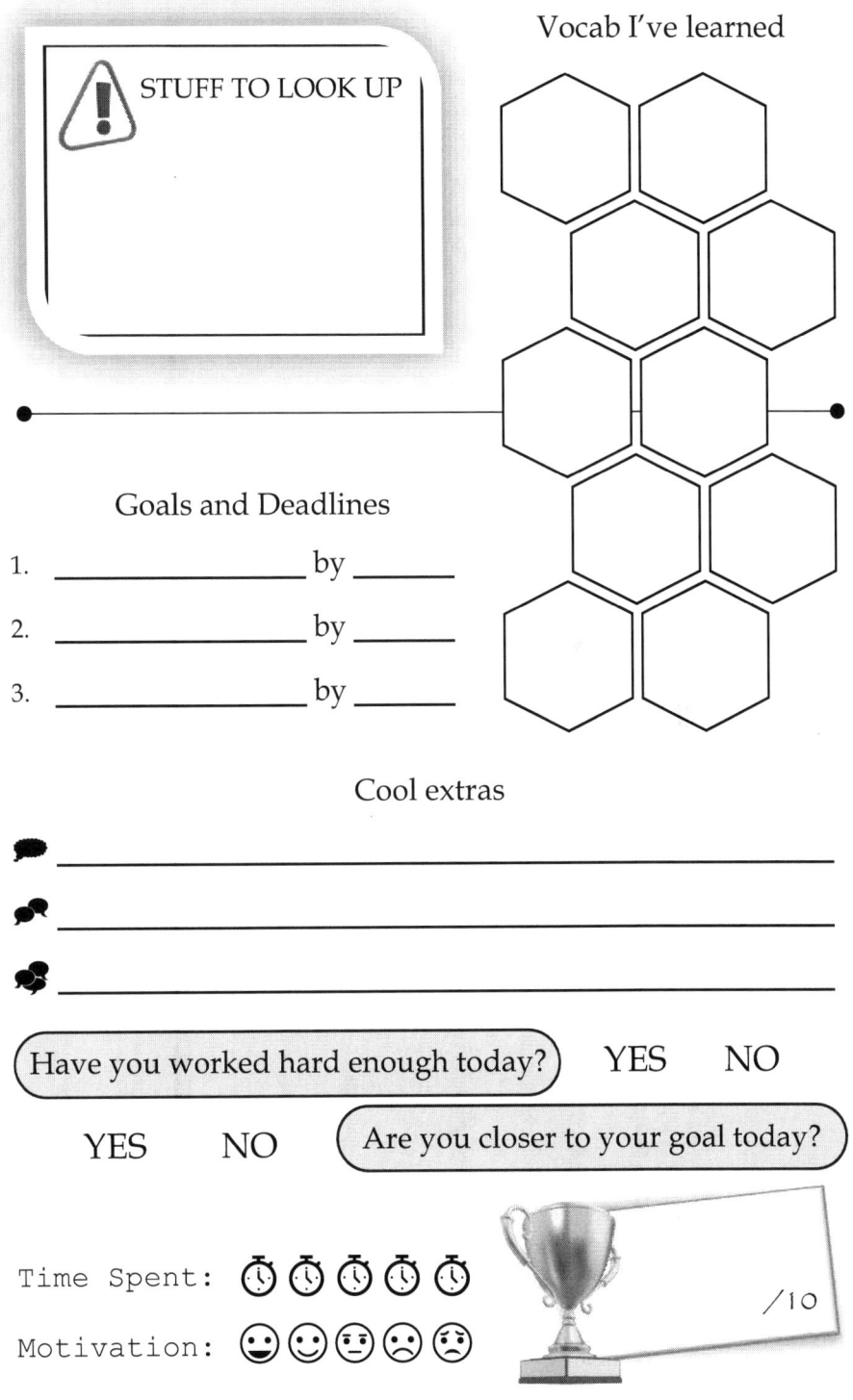

Successful entrepreneurs are givers and not takers of positive energy
ANONYMOUS

Today's work

Active Passive

☑ _____ ☐ ☐
☑ _____ ☐ ☐
☑ _____ ☐ ☐
☑ _____ ☐ ☐

Things I have memorized

things I still can't remember

Season

Episode

Minute

⁉ Have you forced yourself today to speak the language with someone?   YES   NO

NOTES

_____
_____
_____

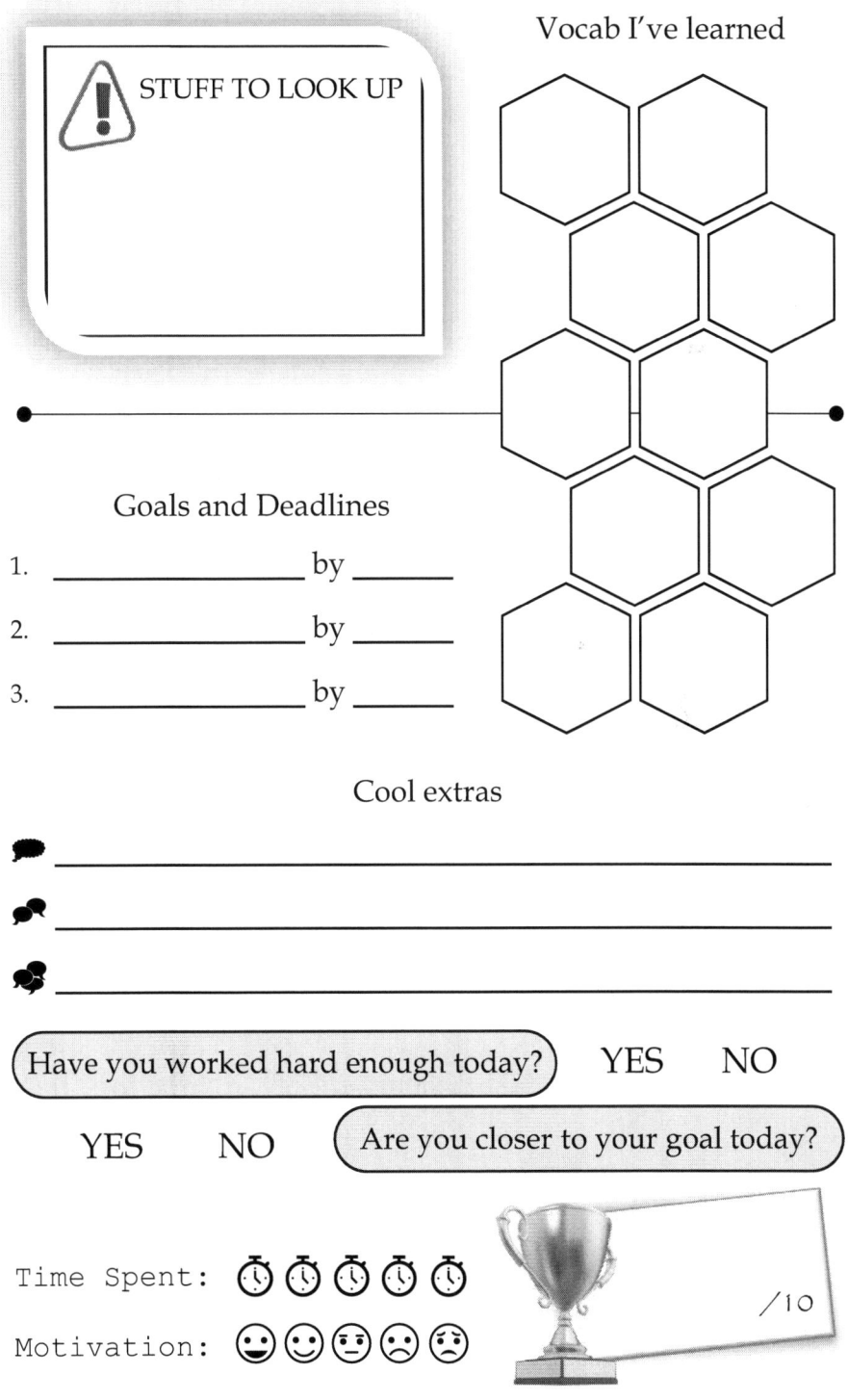

Opportunities don't happen, you create them
CHRIS GROSSER

Today's work

Active Passive

☑ _____ ☐ ☐
☑ _____ ☐ ☐
☑ _____ ☐ ☐
☑ _____ ☐ ☐

Things I have memorized

things I still can't remember

Season

Episode

Minute

‼ Have you forced yourself today to speak the language with someone?   YES   NO

NOTES

_____
_____
_____

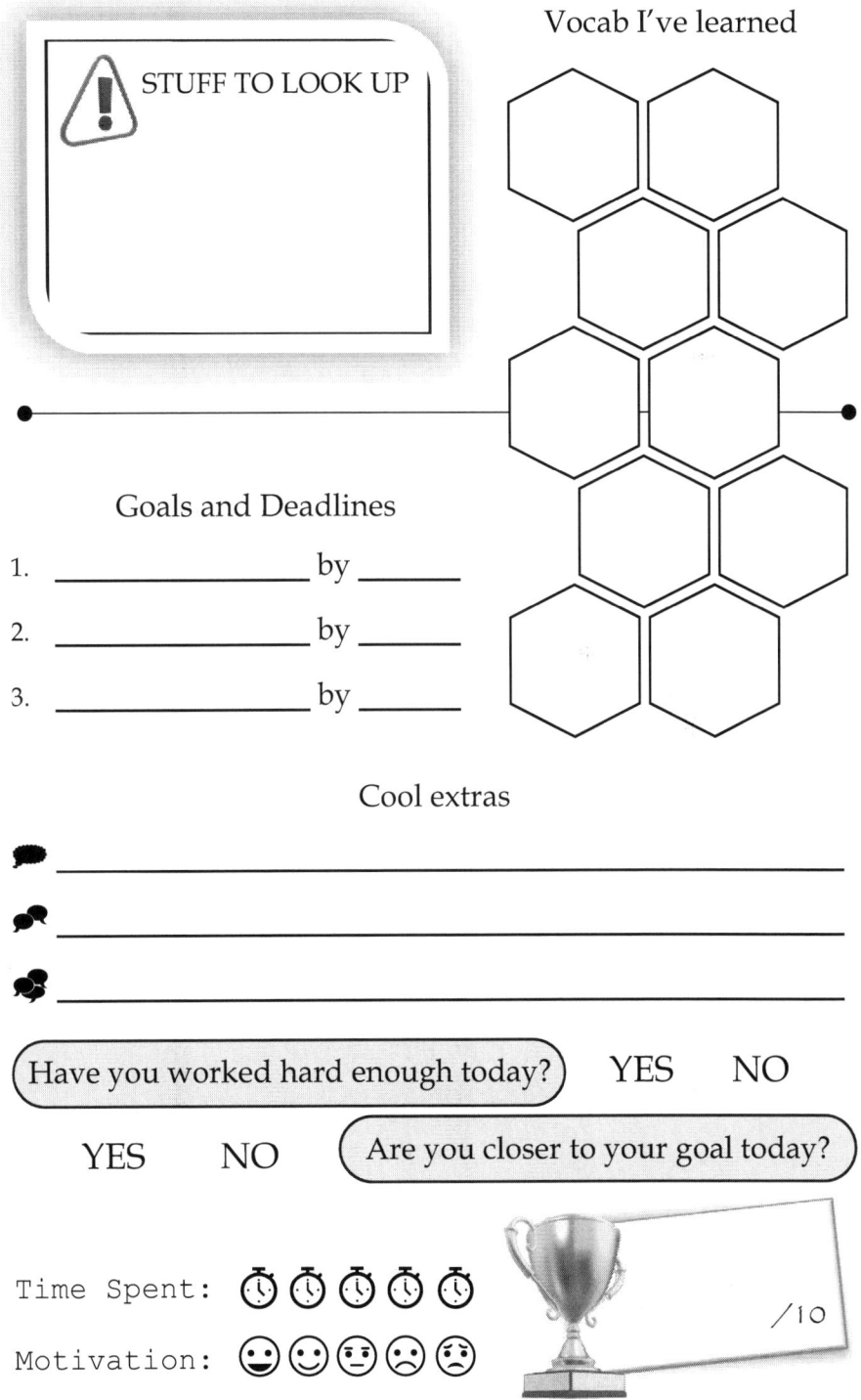

⚠ STUFF TO LOOK UP

Vocab I've learned

Goals and Deadlines

1. _____ by ____
2. _____ by ____
3. _____ by ____

Cool extras

💬 _____
💬 _____
💬 _____

(Have you worked hard enough today?)   YES   NO

YES   NO   (Are you closer to your goal today?)

Time Spent: ⏱ ⏱ ⏱ ⏱ ⏱

Motivation: 😃 🙂 😐 🙁 😣

/10

Try not to become a person of success, but rather try to become a person of value
ALBERT EINSTEIN

Today's work

Active Passive

- ☑ _____ ☐ ☐
- ☑ _____ ☐ ☐
- ☑ _____ ☐ ☐
- ☑ _____ ☐ ☐

Things I have memorized

things I still can't remember

Season

Episode

Minute

⁉ Have you forced yourself today to speak the language with someone?   YES   NO

NOTES

_____

_____

_____

⚠ STUFF TO LOOK UP

Vocab I've learned

Goals and Deadlines

1. _____ by _____
2. _____ by _____
3. _____ by _____

Cool extras

💬 _____
💬 _____
💬 _____

(Have you worked hard enough today?)   YES   NO

YES   NO   (Are you closer to your goal today?)

Time Spent: 🕐 🕐 🕐 🕐 🕐

Motivation: 😊 🙂 😐 🙁 😞

/10

Great minds discuss ideas; average minds discuss events; small minds discuss people
ELEANOR ROOSEVELT

Today's work

Active   Passive

☑ _____   ☐ ☐
☑ _____   ☐ ☐
☑ _____   ☐ ☐
☑ _____   ☐ ☐

Things I have memorized

things I still can't remember

Season

Episode

Minute

⁉ Have you forced yourself today to speak the language with someone?   YES   NO

NOTES

_____
_____
_____

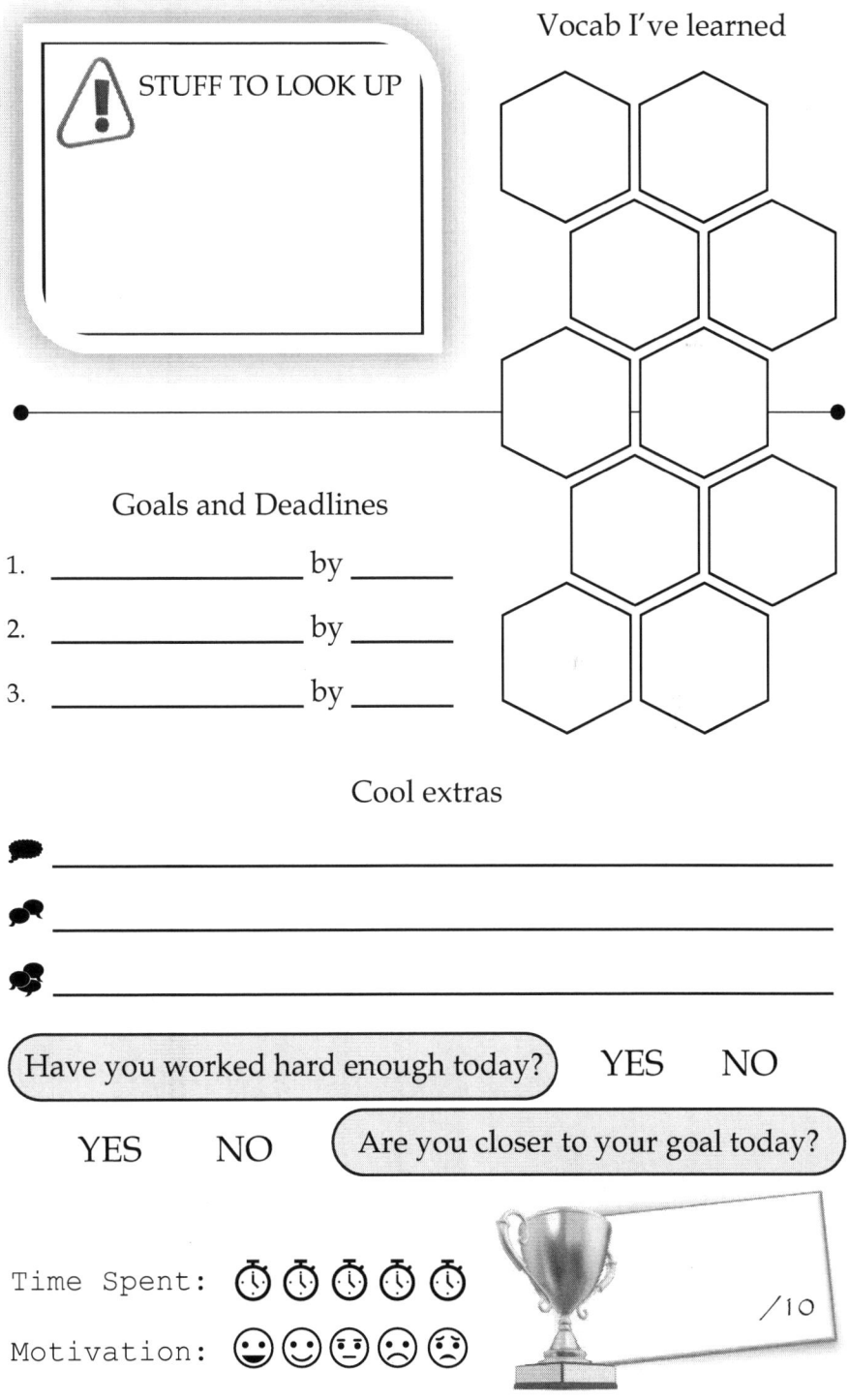

[138]

I have not failed. I've just found 10,000 ways that won't work.
THOMAS A. EDISON

Today's work

Active Passive

☑ _____ ☐ ☐
☑ _____ ☐ ☐
☑ _____ ☐ ☐
☑ _____ ☐ ☐

Things I have memorized

things I still can't remember

Season

Episode

Minute

⁉ Have you forced yourself today to speak the language with someone?   YES   NO

NOTES

_____
_____
_____

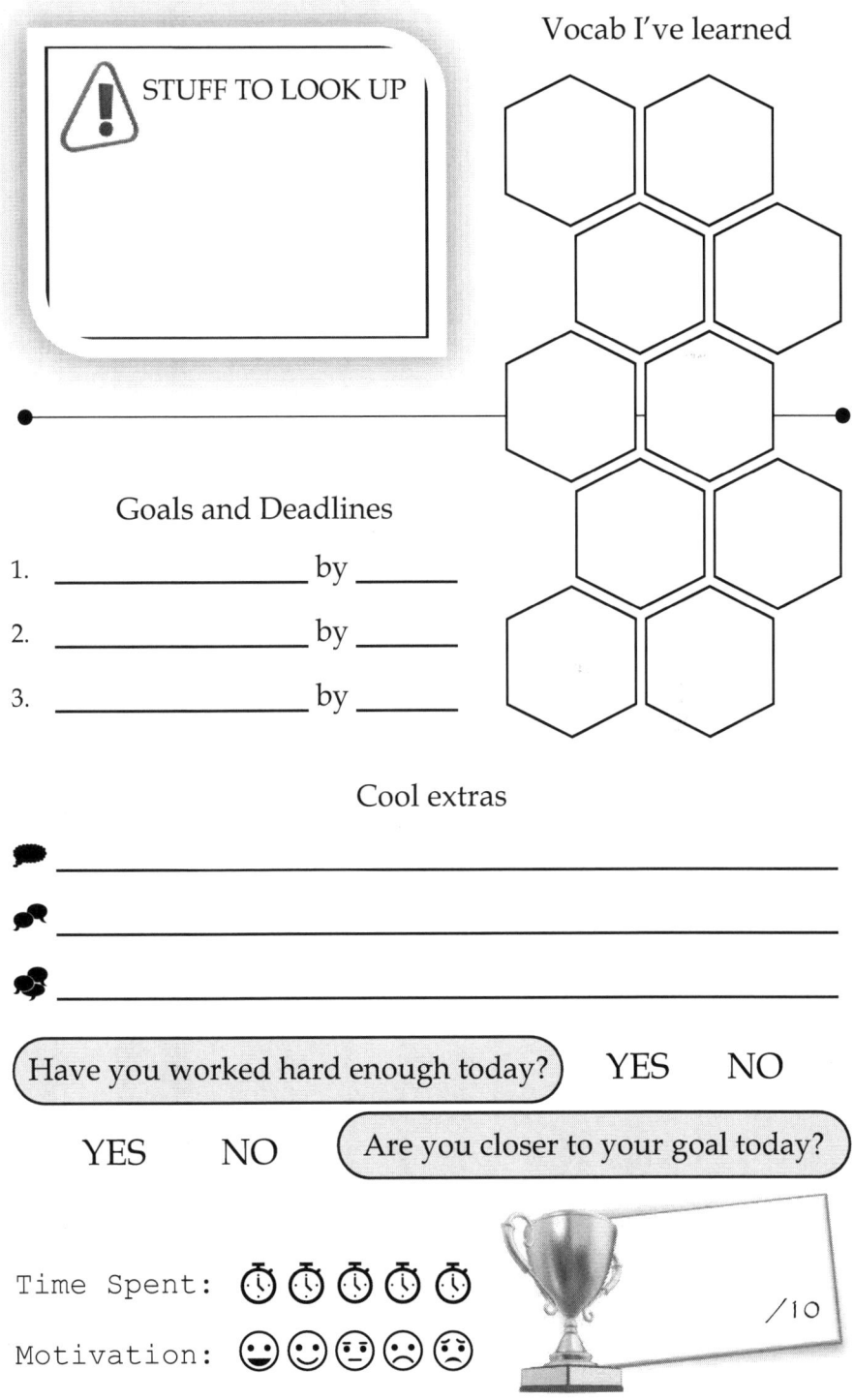

[140]

No one can make you feel inferior without your consent
ELEANOR ROOSEVELT

Today's work   Active Passive

☑ _____   ☐   ☐
☑ _____   ☐   ☐
☑ _____   ☐   ☐
☑ _____   ☐   ☐

Things I have memorized

things I still can't remember

Season
Episode
Minute

‼ Have you forced yourself today to speak the language with someone?   YES   NO

NOTES

_____
_____
_____

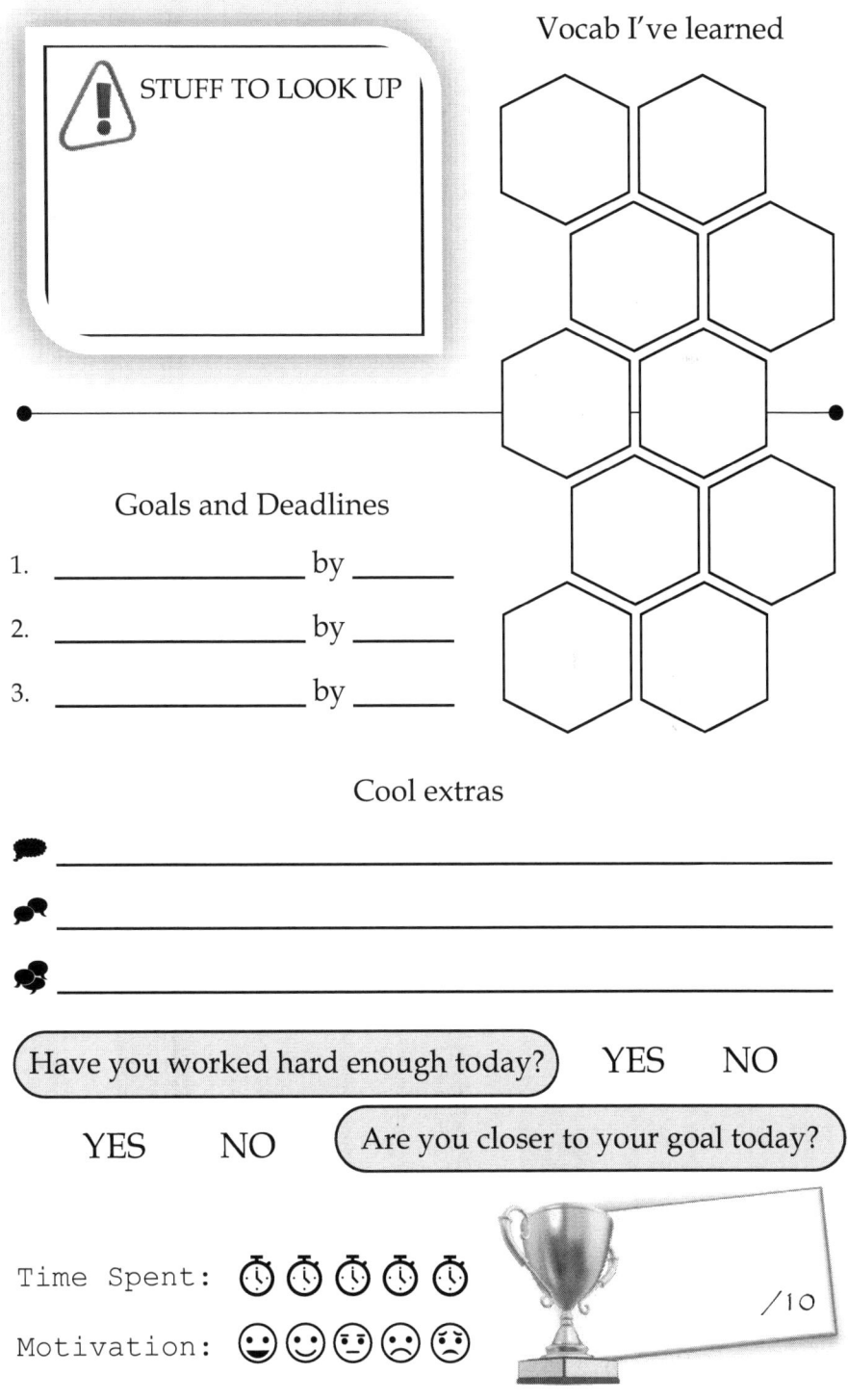

⚠ STUFF TO LOOK UP

Vocab I've learned

Goals and Deadlines

1. _____ by _____
2. _____ by _____
3. _____ by _____

Cool extras

🗨 _____
🗨 _____
🗨 _____

Have you worked hard enough today?　　YES　　NO

YES　　NO　　Are you closer to your goal today?

Time Spent: ⏱ ⏱ ⏱ ⏱ ⏱

Motivation: 😃 🙂 😐 🙁 😣

/10

If you're going through hell keep going
WINSTON CHURCHILL

Today's work

                                                                                  Active Passive

- ☑ _____ ☐ ☐
- ☑ _____ ☐ ☐
- ☑ _____ ☐ ☐
- ☑ _____ ☐ ☐

Things I have memorized

things I still can't remember

Season

Episode

Minute

!? Have you forced yourself today to speak the language with someone?   YES   NO

NOTES

_____

_____

_____

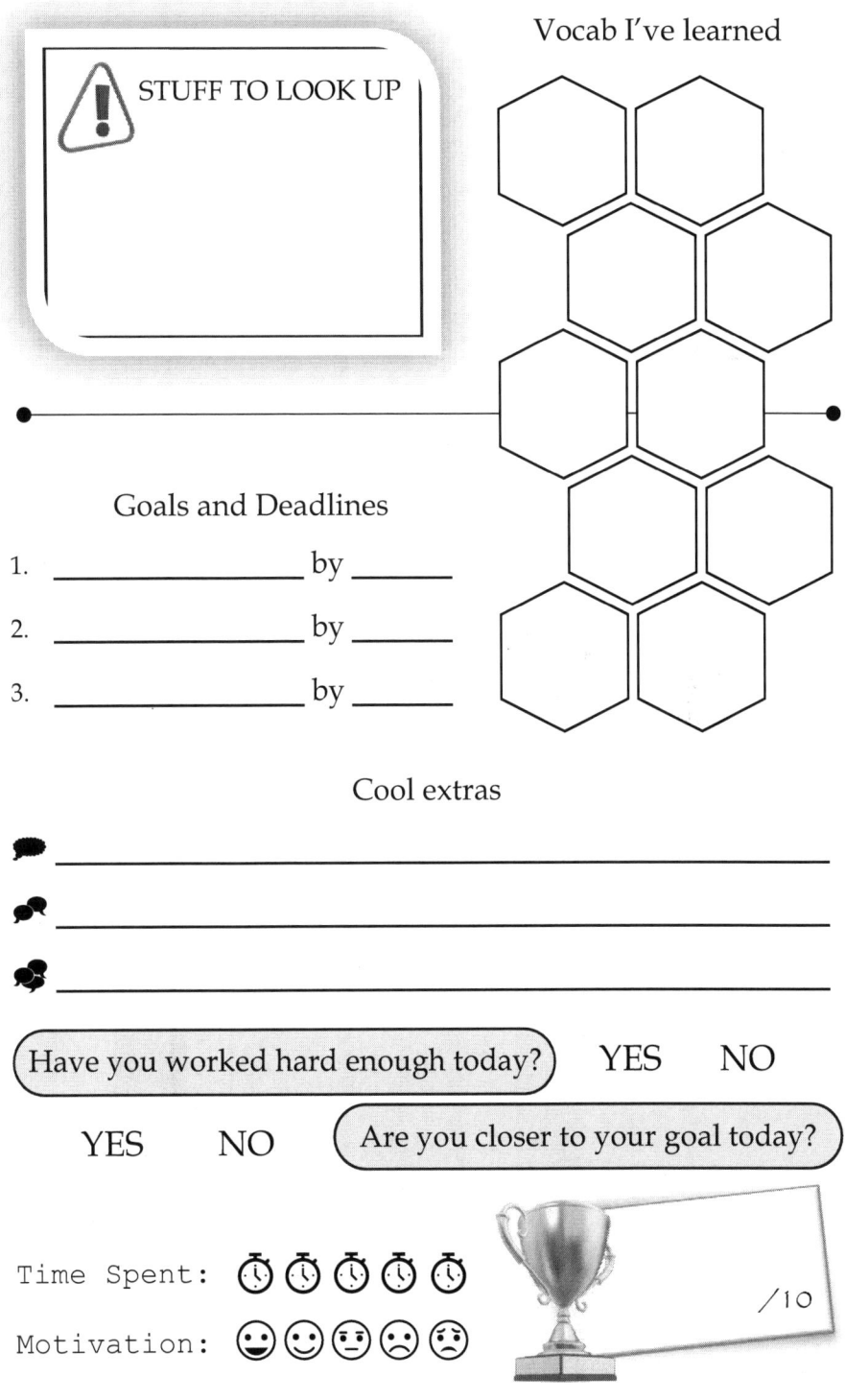

[144]

What seems to us as bitter trials are often blessings in disguise
OSCAR WILDE

Today's work

Active Passive

☑ _____ ☐ ☐
☑ _____ ☐ ☐
☑ _____ ☐ ☐
☑ _____ ☐ ☐

Things I have memorized

things I still can't remember

Season
Episode
Minute

!? Have you forced yourself today to speak the language with someone?   YES   NO

NOTES

_____
_____
_____

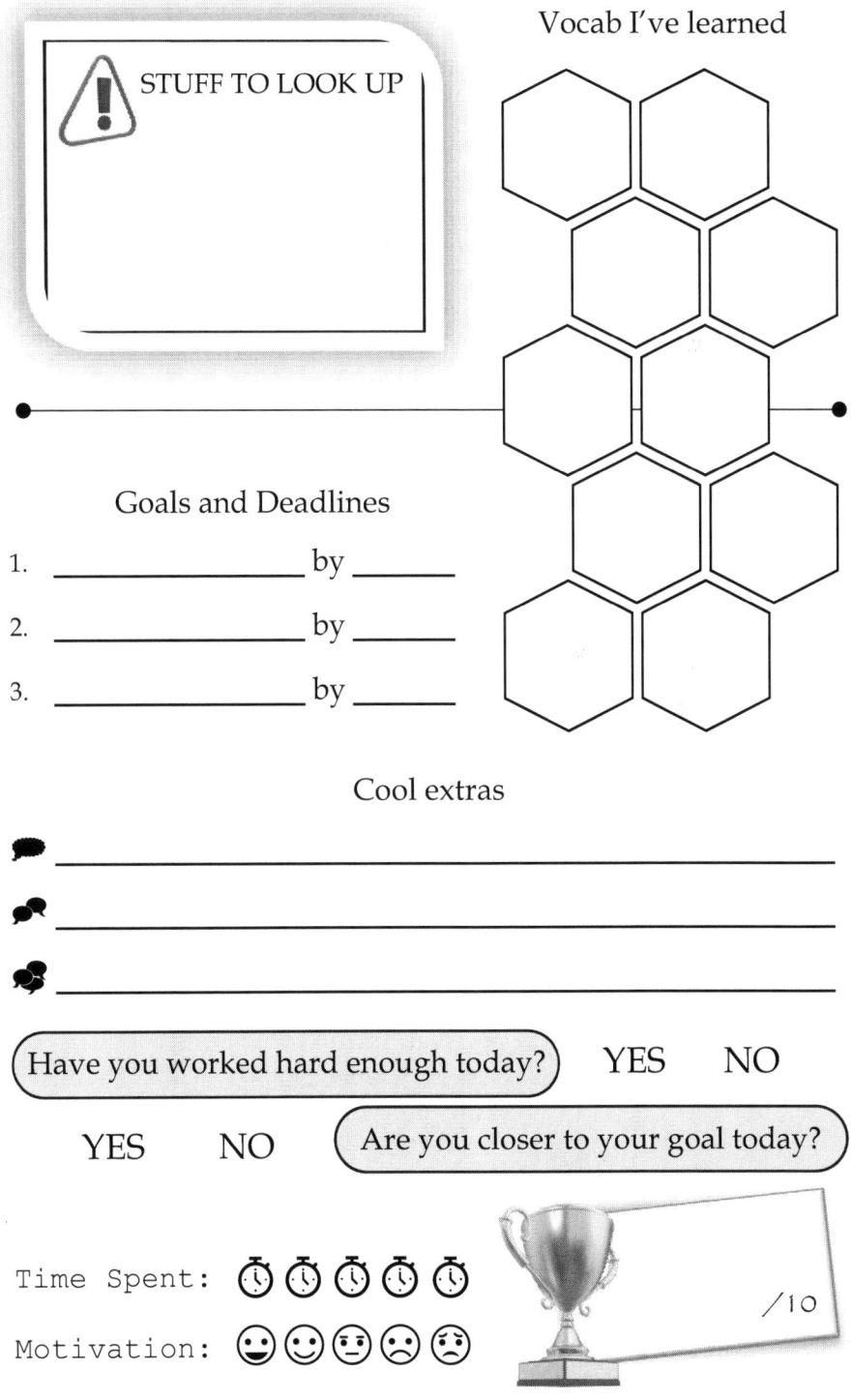

[146]

The meaning of life is to find your gift. The purpose of life is to give it away
ANONYMOUS

Today's work

Active Passive

☑ _____ ☐ ☐
☑ _____ ☐ ☐
☑ _____ ☐ ☐
☑ _____ ☐ ☐

Things I have memorized

things I still can't remember

Season

Episode

Minute

⁉ Have you forced yourself today to speak the language with someone?   YES   NO

NOTES

_____
_____
_____

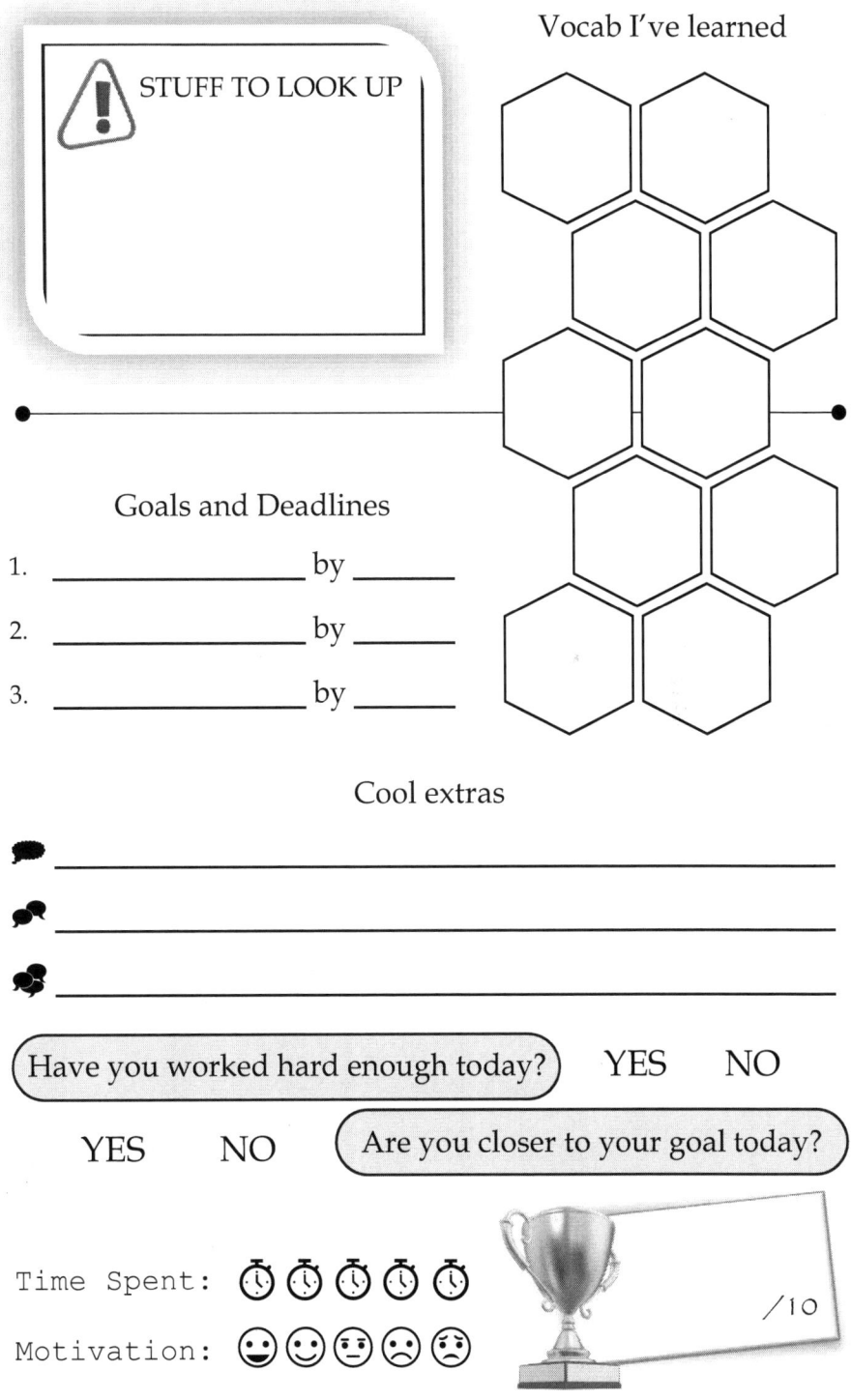

STUFF TO LOOK UP

Vocab I've learned

Goals and Deadlines

1. _____ by _____
2. _____ by _____
3. _____ by _____

Cool extras

● _____
● _____
● _____

Have you worked hard enough today?   YES   NO

YES   NO   Are you closer to your goal today?

Time Spent:
Motivation:

/10

The distance between insanity and genius is measured only by success
BRUCE FEIRSTEIN

Today's work   Active Passive

☑ _____   ☐ ☐
☑ _____   ☐ ☐
☑ _____   ☐ ☐
☑ _____   ☐ ☐

Things I have memorized

things I still can't remember

Season

Episode

Minute

⁉ Have you forced yourself today to speak the language with someone?   YES   NO

NOTES

_____
_____
_____

⚠️ STUFF TO LOOK UP

Vocab I've learned

Goals and Deadlines

1. _____ by _____
2. _____ by _____
3. _____ by _____

Cool extras

💭 _____
💭 _____
💭 _____

Have you worked hard enough today?   YES   NO

YES   NO   Are you closer to your goal today?

Time Spent: ⏱ ⏱ ⏱ ⏱ ⏱
Motivation: 😃 🙂 😐 ☹️ 😣

/10

Don't be afraid to give up the good to go for the great
JOHN D. ROCKEFELLER

Today's work

Active Passive

☑ _____ ☐ ☐
☑ _____ ☐ ☐
☑ _____ ☐ ☐
☑ _____ ☐ ☐

Things I have memorized

things I still can't remember

Season

Episode

Minute

⁉ Have you forced yourself today to speak the language with someone?   YES   NO

NOTES

_____
_____
_____

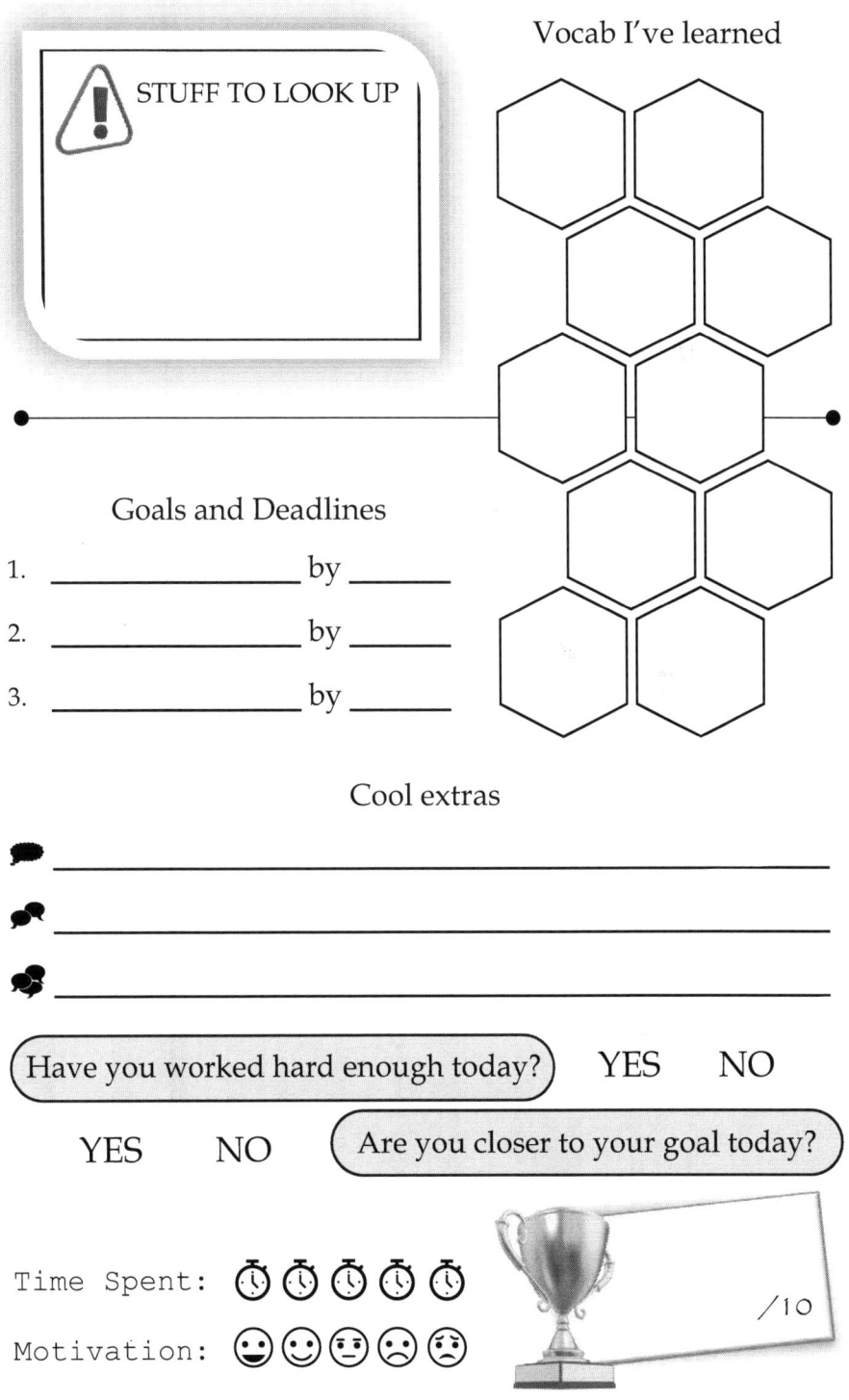

No masterpiece was ever created by a lazy artist
ANONYMOUS

Today's work

Active Passive

- [x] _____ ☐ ☐
- [x] _____ ☐ ☐
- [x] _____ ☐ ☐
- [x] _____ ☐ ☐

↑ Things I have memorized

• •
• •
• •

things I still can't remember ↓

Season

Episode

Minute

⁉ Have you forced yourself today to speak the language with someone?   YES   NO

NOTES

_____

_____

_____

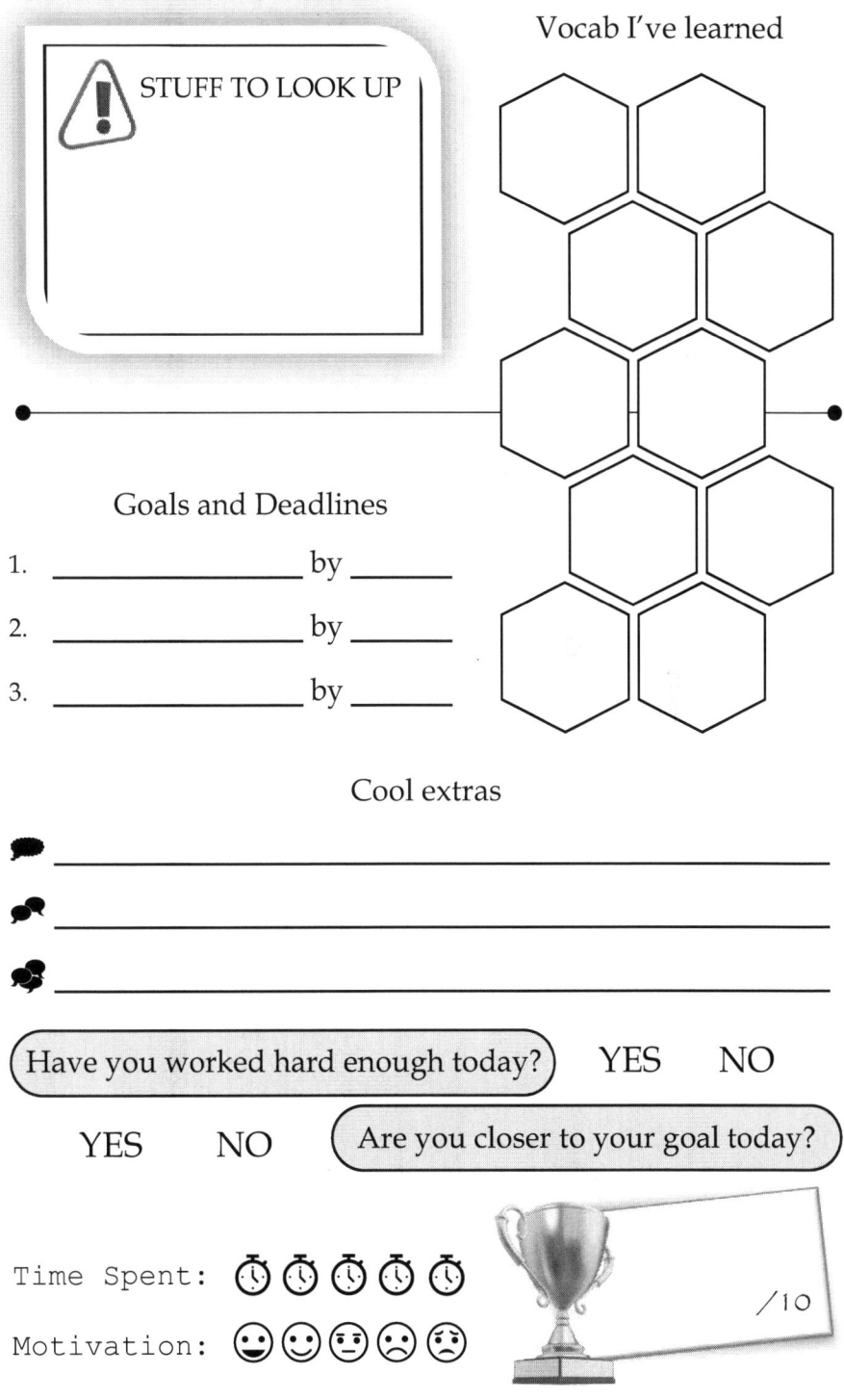

If you can't explain it simply, you don't understand it well enough
ALBERT EINSTEIN

Today's work

Active Passive

☑ _____ ☐ ☐

☑ _____ ☐ ☐

☑ _____ ☐ ☐

☑ _____ ☐ ☐

Things I have memorized

things I still can't remember

Season

Episode

Minute

Have you forced yourself today to speak the language with someone? YES   NO

NOTES

_____

_____

_____

⚠ STUFF TO LOOK UP

Vocab I've learned

Goals and Deadlines

1. _____ by _____
2. _____ by _____
3. _____ by _____

Cool extras

💬 _____
💬 _____
💬 _____

(Have you worked hard enough today?)   YES   NO

YES   NO   (Are you closer to your goal today?)

Time Spent: ⏱ ⏱ ⏱ ⏱ ⏱
Motivation: 😀 🙂 😐 🙁 😣

/10

Do one thing every day that scares you
ANONYMOUS

Today's work

Active   Passive

☑ _____   ☐   ☐
☑ _____   ☐   ☐
☑ _____   ☐   ☐
☑ _____   ☐   ☐

Things I have memorized

things I still can't remember

Season

Episode

Minute

⁉ Have you forced yourself today to speak the language with someone?   YES   NO

NOTES

_____
_____
_____

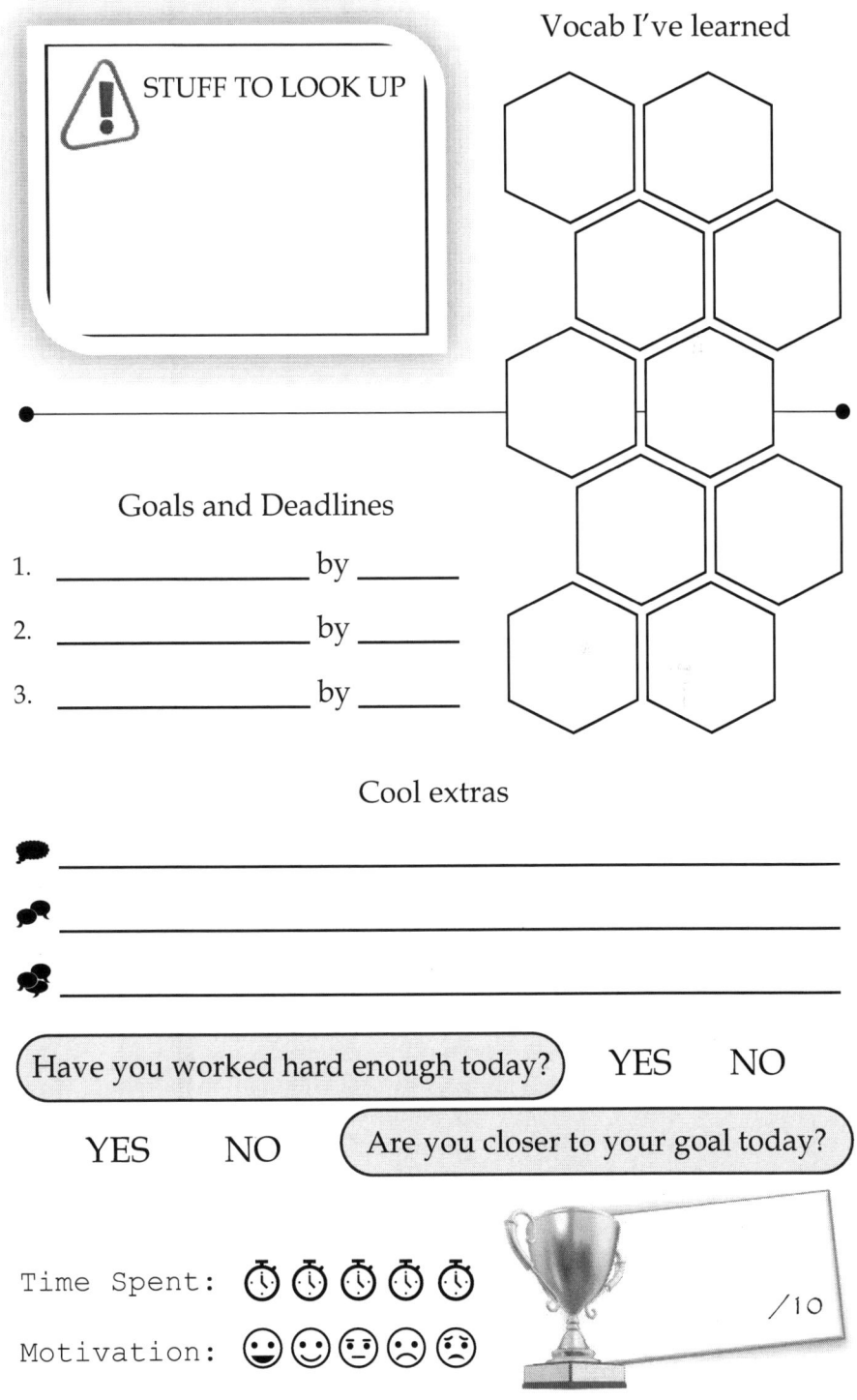

[158]

Life is not about finding yourself. Life is about creating yourself
LOLLY DASKAL

Today's work

Active Passive

☑ _____ ☐ ☐
☑ _____ ☐ ☐
☑ _____ ☐ ☐
☑ _____ ☐ ☐

Things I have memorized

things I still can't remember

Season

Episode

Minute

⁉ Have you forced yourself today to speak the language with someone?   YES   NO

NOTES

_____
_____
_____

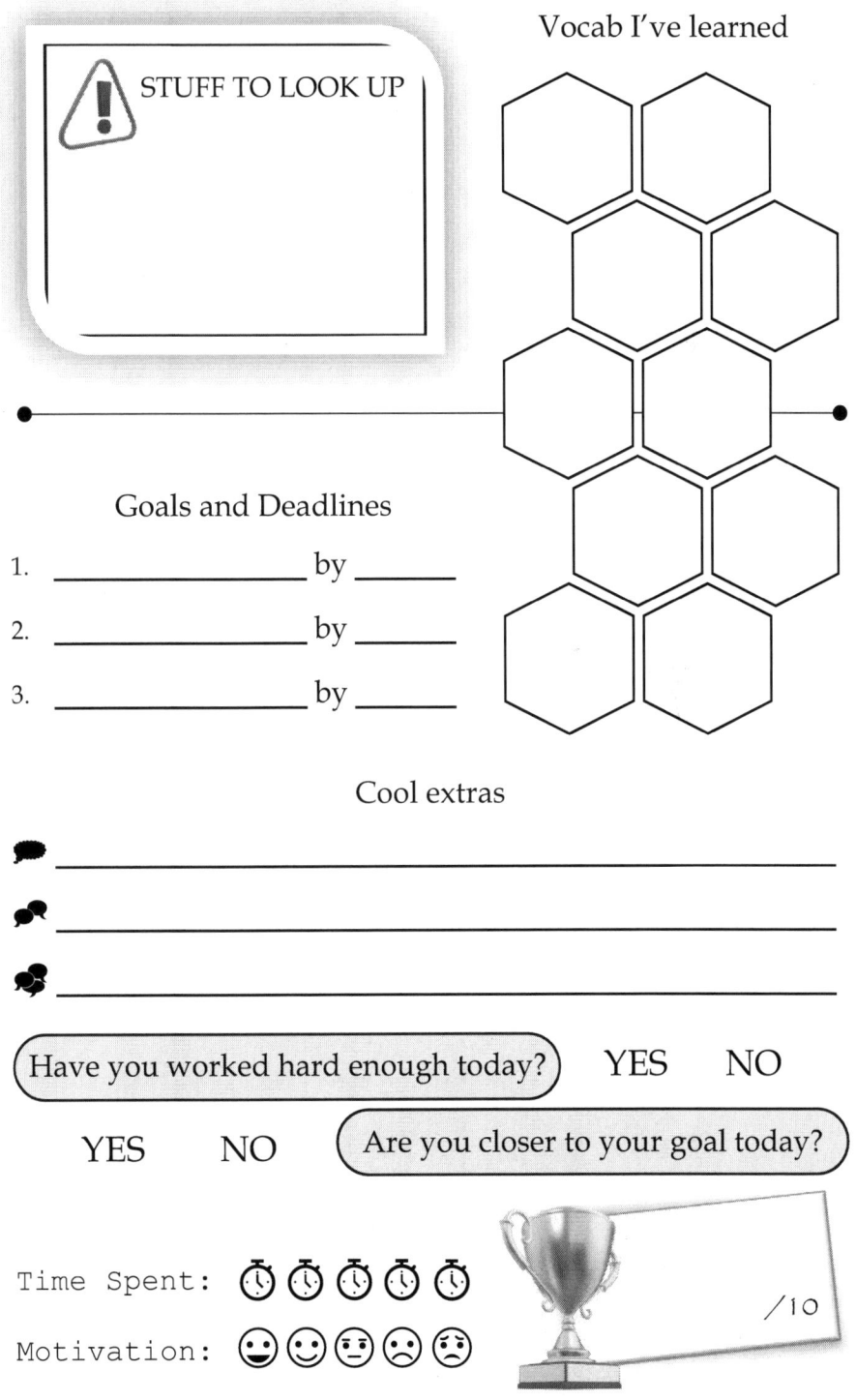

Nothing in the world is more common than unsuccessful people with talent
ANONYMOUS

Today's work

Active Passive

☑ _____ ☐ ☐
☑ _____ ☐ ☐
☑ _____ ☐ ☐
☑ _____ ☐ ☐

Things I have memorized

things I still can't remember

Season

Episode

Minute

⁉ Have you forced yourself today to speak the language with someone?   YES   NO

NOTES

_____
_____
_____

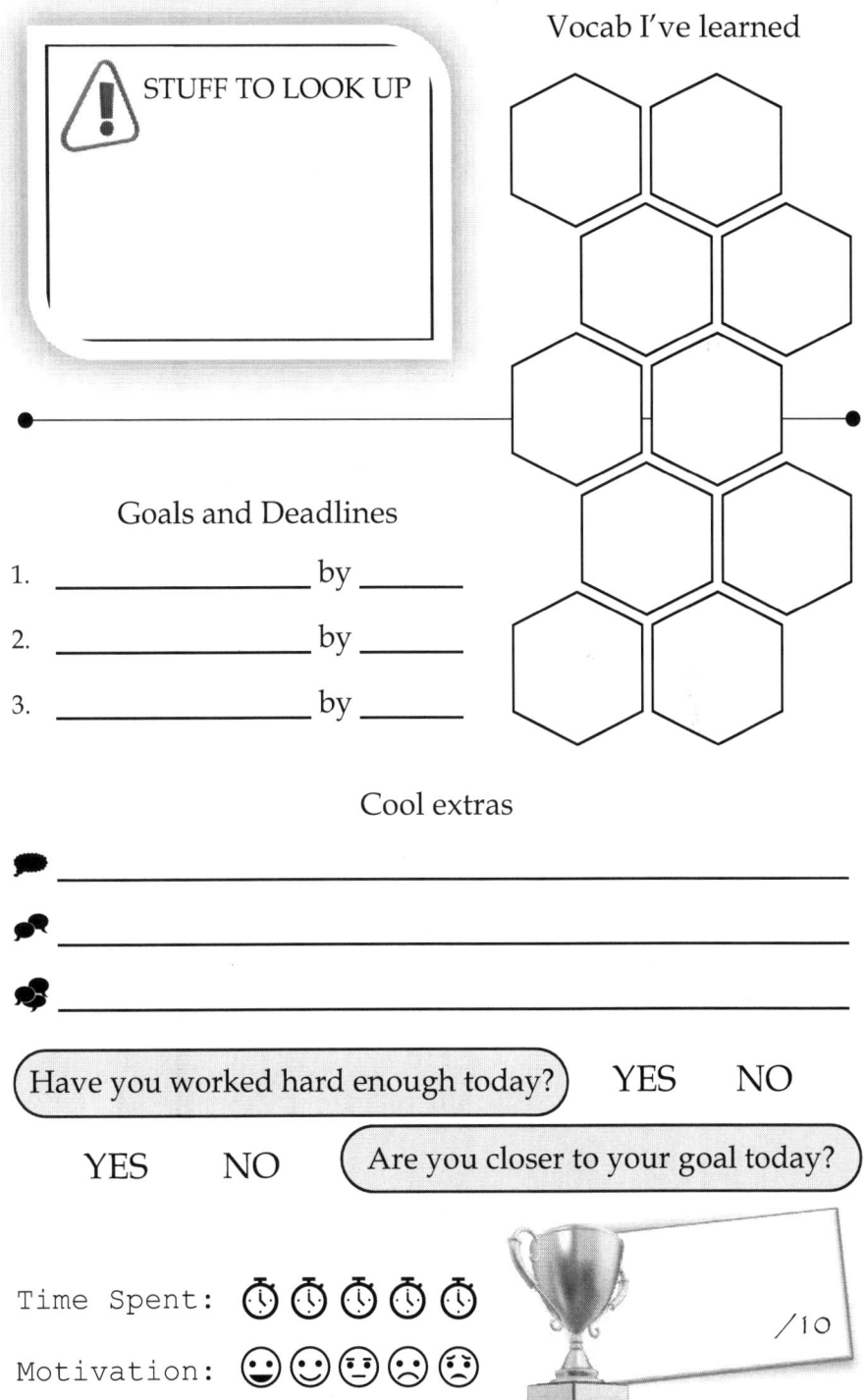

You can do anything, but not everything
ANONYMOUS

Today's work

Active Passive

- ☑ _____ ☐ ☐
- ☑ _____ ☐ ☐
- ☑ _____ ☐ ☐
- ☑ _____ ☐ ☐

Things I have memorized

things I still can't remember

Season

Episode

Minute

⁉ Have you forced yourself today to speak the language with someone?   YES   NO

NOTES

_____
_____
_____

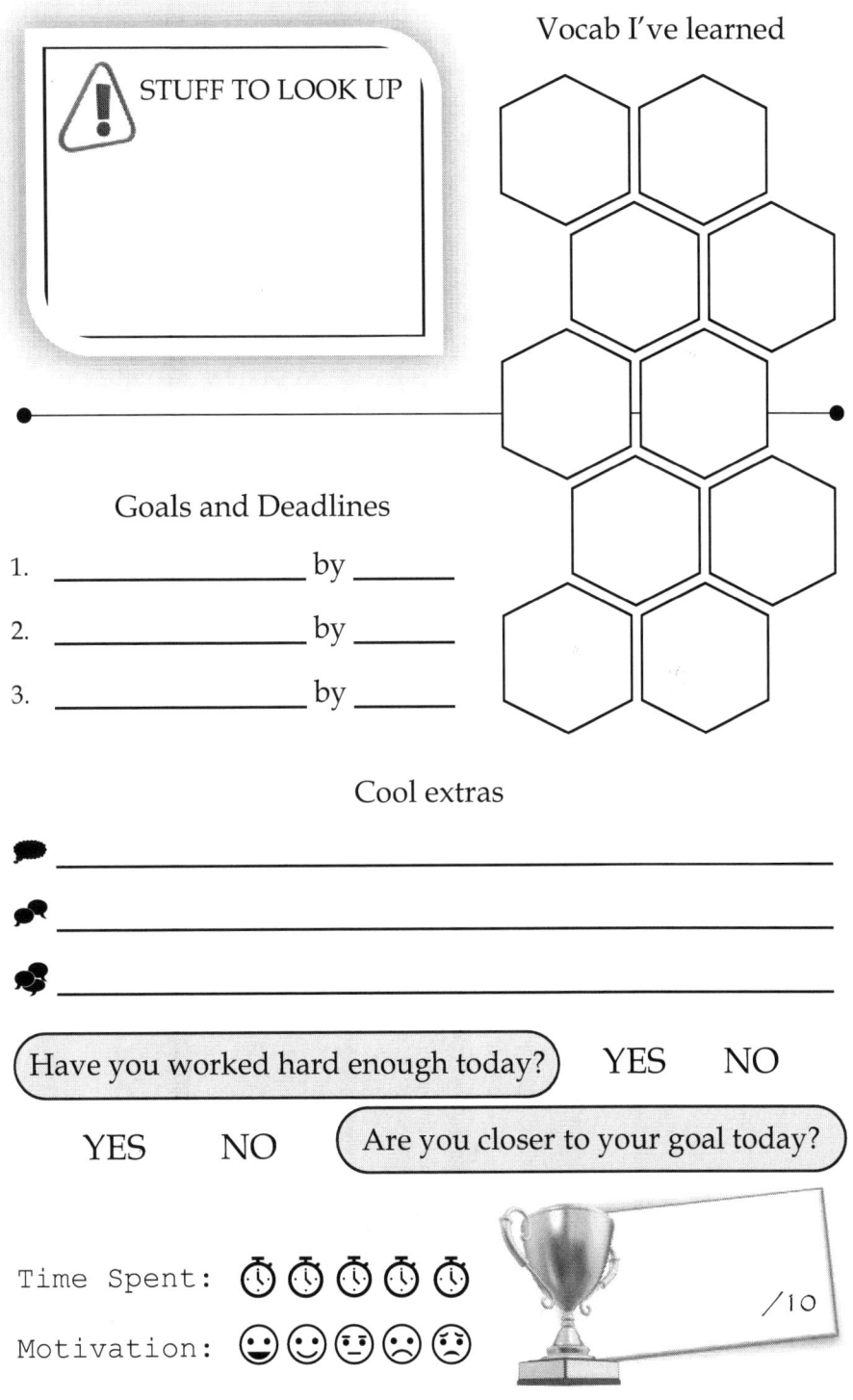

⚠ STUFF TO LOOK UP

Vocab I've learned

Goals and Deadlines

1. _____ by _____
2. _____ by _____
3. _____ by _____

Cool extras

🗨 _____
🗨 _____
🗨 _____

(Have you worked hard enough today?)   YES   NO

   YES   NO   (Are you closer to your goal today?)

Time Spent: 🕐 🕐 🕐 🕐 🕐
Motivation: 🙂 🙂 😐 🙁 😣

/10

Innovation distinguishes between a leader and a follower
STEVE JOBS

Today's work

Active Passive

☑ _____ ☐ ☐
☑ _____ ☐ ☐
☑ _____ ☐ ☐
☑ _____ ☐ ☐

Things I have memorized

things I still can't remember

Season

Episode

Minute

⁉ Have you forced yourself today to speak the language with someone? YES   NO

NOTES

_____
_____
_____

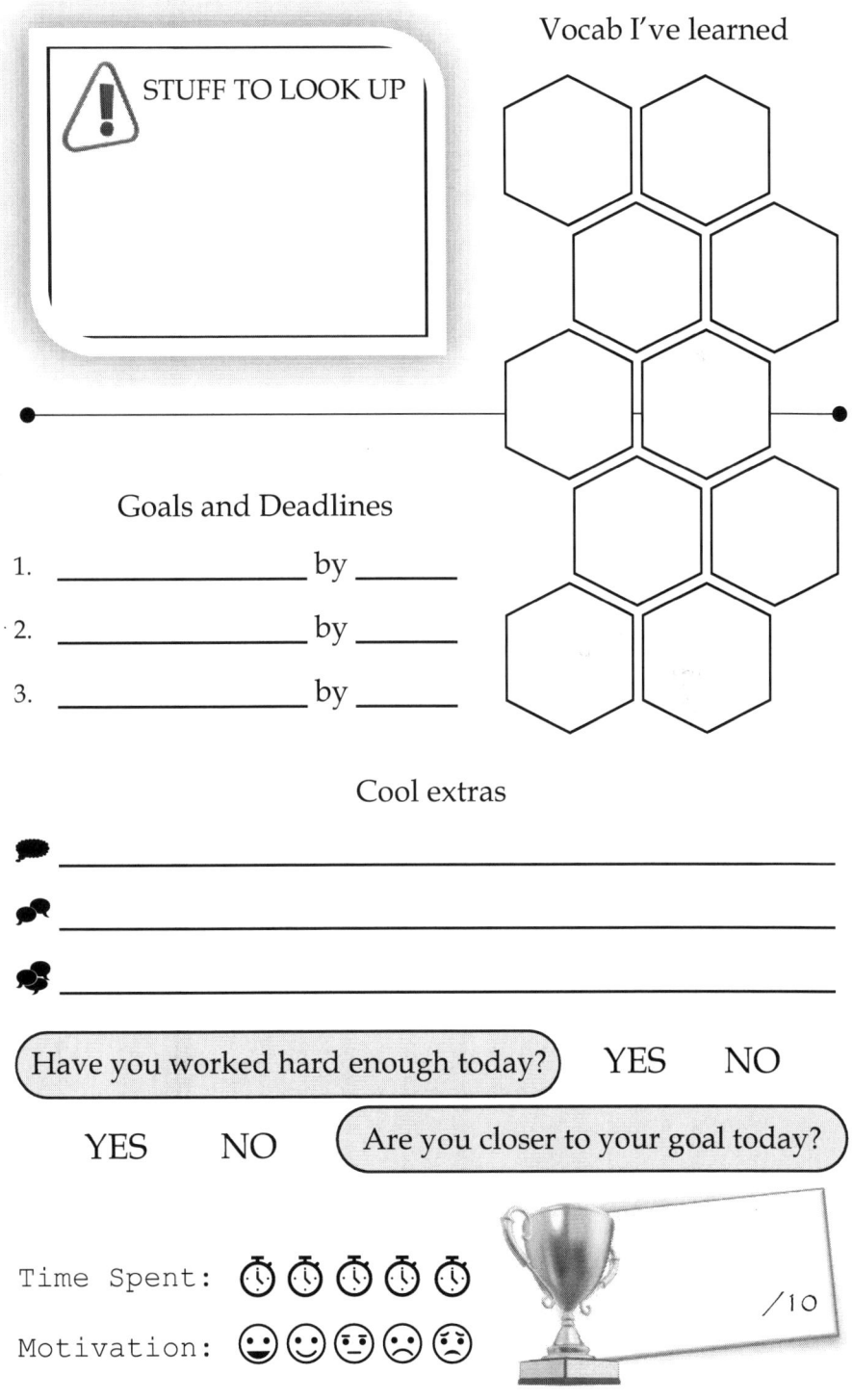

STUFF TO LOOK UP

Vocab I've learned

Goals and Deadlines

1. _____ by _____
2. _____ by _____
3. _____ by _____

Cool extras

- _____
- _____
- _____

Have you worked hard enough today?   YES   NO

YES   NO   Are you closer to your goal today?

Time Spent: 🕐 🕐 🕐 🕐 🕐

Motivation: 😊 🙂 😐 🙁 😣

/10

[📅] [   ]   [   ] [🏆]

I find that the harder I work, the more luck I seem to have
THOMAS JEFFERSON

Today's work

Active Passive

☑ _____ ☐ ☐
☑ _____ ☐ ☐
☑ _____ ☐ ☐
☑ _____ ☐ ☐

⬆ Things I have memorized

•   •
•   •
•   •

things I still can't remember ⬇

Season

Episode

Minute

‼⁉ Have you forced yourself today to speak the language with someone?   YES   NO

NOTES

_____

_____

_____

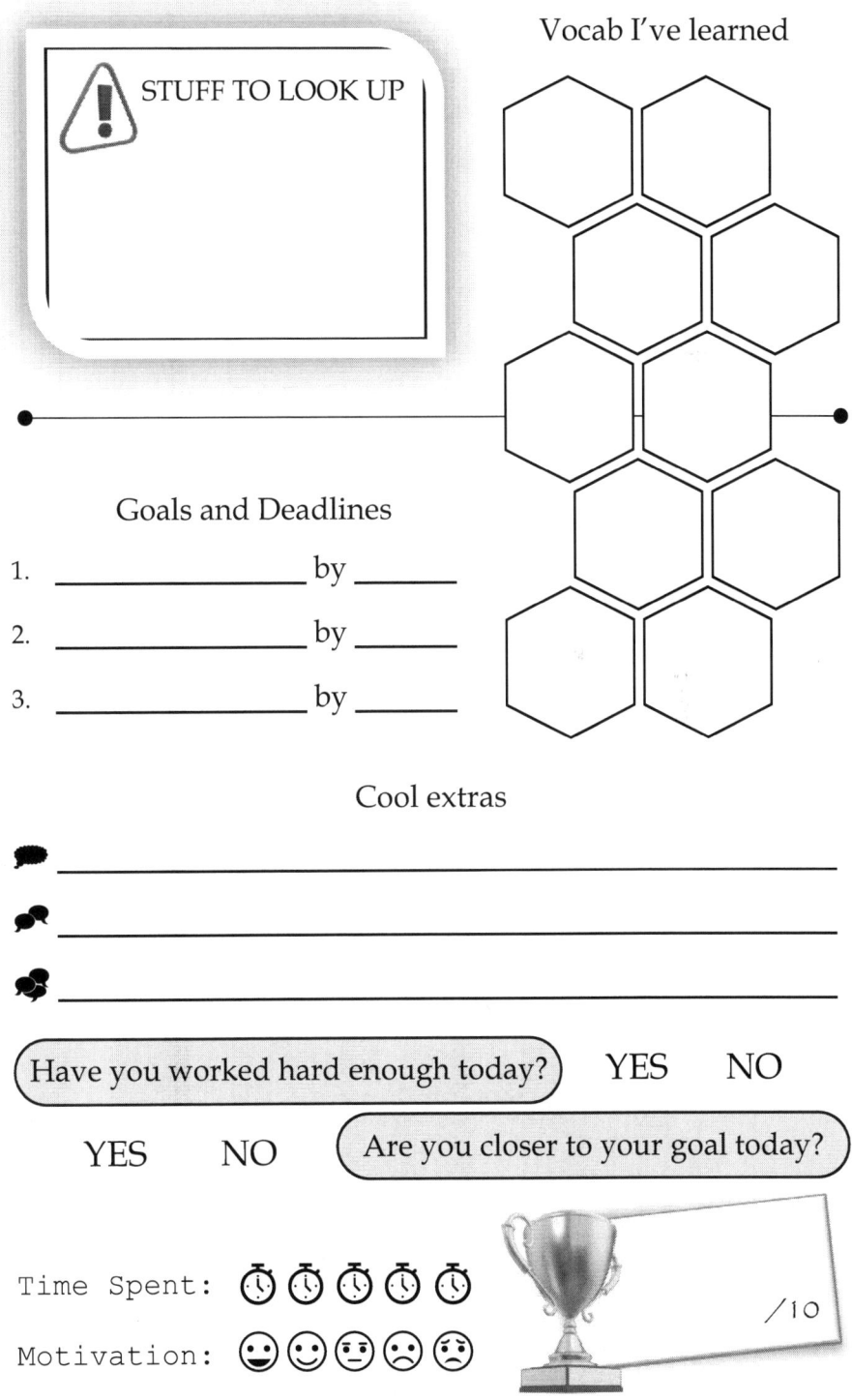

[168]

The starting point of all achievement is desire
NAPOLEON HILL

Today's work

Active Passive

☑ _____ ☐ ☐
☑ _____ ☐ ☐
☑ _____ ☐ ☐
☑ _____ ☐ ☐

Things I have memorized

things I still can't remember

Season

Episode

Minute

⚠ Have you forced yourself today to speak the language with someone?   YES   NO

NOTES

_____
_____
_____

⚠ STUFF TO LOOK UP

Vocab I've learned

Goals and Deadlines

1. _____ by _____
2. _____ by _____
3. _____ by _____

Cool extras

💬 _____
💬 _____
💬 _____

(Have you worked hard enough today?)   YES   NO

YES   NO   (Are you closer to your goal today?)

Time Spent: ⏱ ⏱ ⏱ ⏱ ⏱

Motivation: 😊 🙂 😐 🙁 😣

/10

Success is the sum of small efforts, repeated day-in and day-out
ROBERT COLLIER

Today's work

Active Passive

- ☑ _____ ☐ ☐
- ☑ _____ ☐ ☐
- ☑ _____ ☐ ☐
- ☑ _____ ☐ ☐

Things I have memorized

things I still can't remember

Season

Episode

Minute

⁉ Have you forced yourself today to speak the language with someone?   YES   NO

NOTES

_____
_____
_____

STUFF TO LOOK UP

Vocab I've learned

Goals and Deadlines

1. _____ by _____
2. _____ by _____
3. _____ by _____

Cool extras

- _____
- _____
- _____

Have you worked hard enough today?   YES   NO

YES   NO   Are you closer to your goal today?

Time Spent: 🕐 🕐 🕐 🕐 🕐

Motivation: 😀 🙂 😐 🙁 😣

/10

All progress takes place outside the comfort zone

MICHAEL JOHN BOBAK

Today's work

Active Passive

☑ _____ ☐ ☐
☑ _____ ☐ ☐
☑ _____ ☐ ☐
☑ _____ ☐ ☐

Things I have memorized

things I still can't remember

Season

Episode

Minute

‼⁇ Have you forced yourself today to speak the language with someone?   YES   NO

NOTES

_____

_____

_____

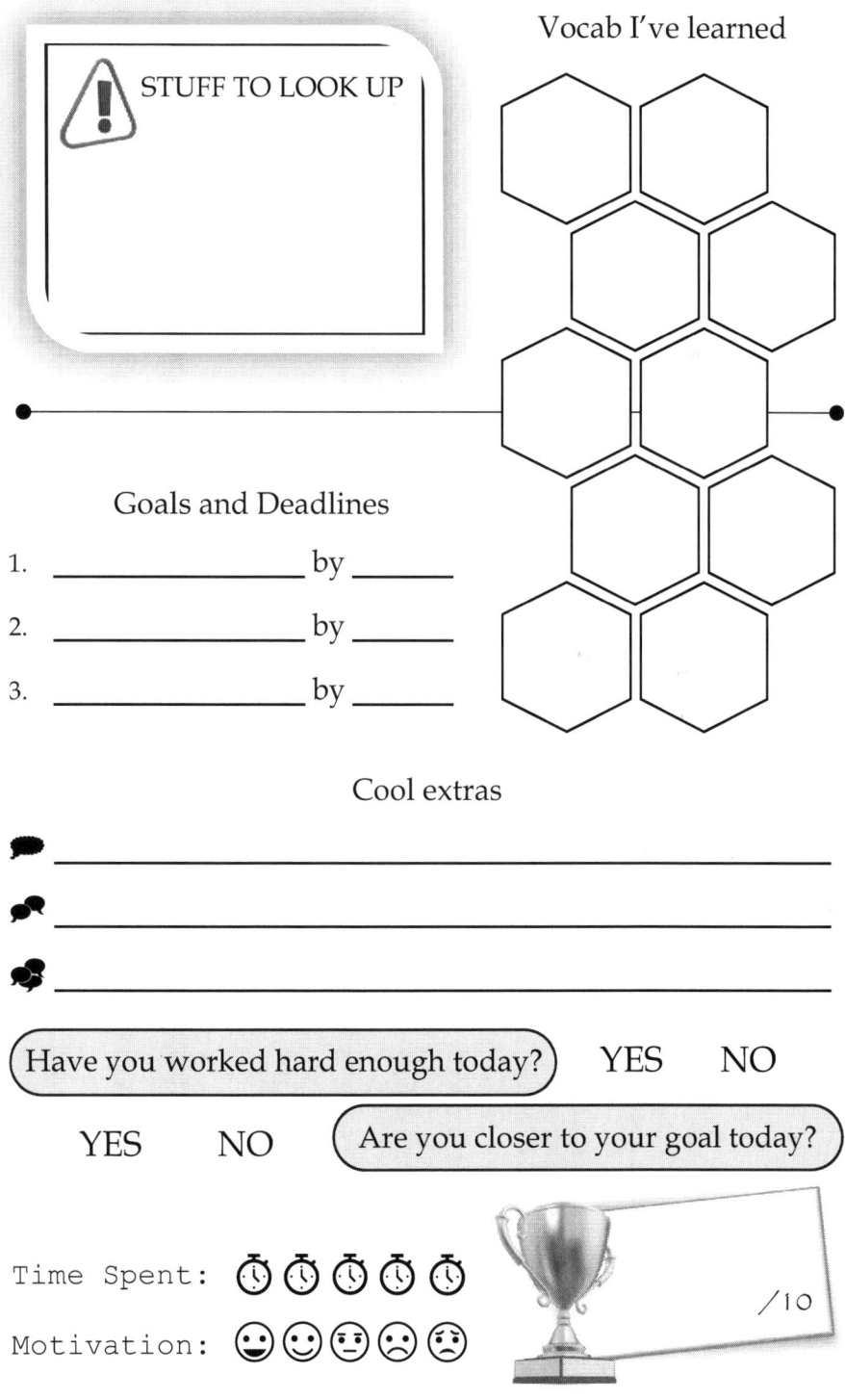

STUFF TO LOOK UP

Vocab I've learned

Goals and Deadlines

1. _____ by _____
2. _____ by _____
3. _____ by _____

Cool extras

💭 _____
💭 _____
💭 _____

Have you worked hard enough today?   YES   NO

YES   NO   Are you closer to your goal today?

Time Spent: ⏱ ⏱ ⏱ ⏱ ⏱

Motivation: 😀 🙂 😐 🙁 😣

/10

Courage is resistance to fear, mastery of fear - not absense of fear
MARK TWAIN

Today's work

Active Passive

☑ _____ ☐ ☐
☑ _____ ☐ ☐
☑ _____ ☐ ☐
☑ _____ ☐ ☐

Things I have memorized

things I still can't remember

Season

Episode

Minute

Have you forced yourself today to speak the language with someone?   YES   NO

NOTES

_____
_____
_____

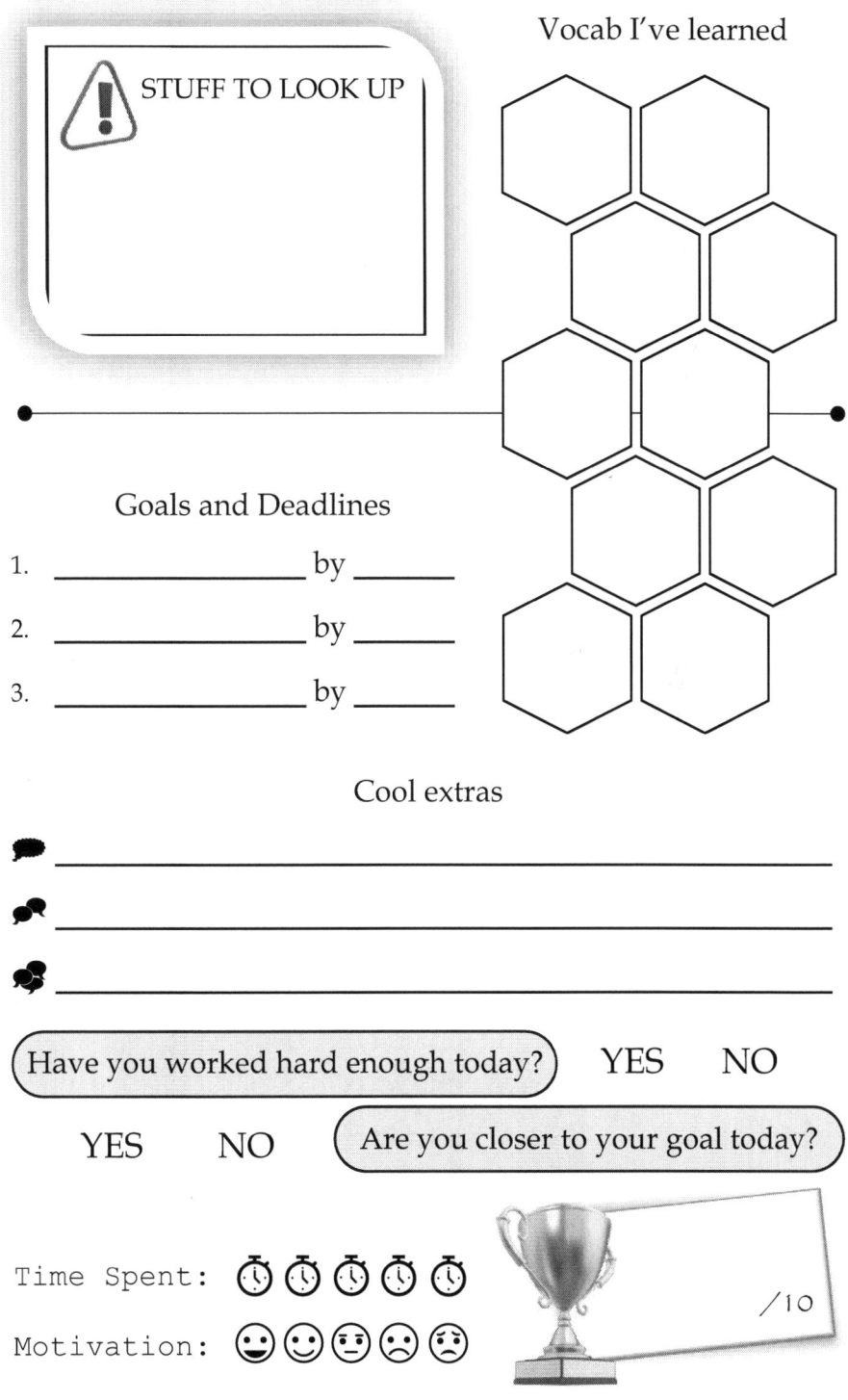

⚠ STUFF TO LOOK UP

Vocab I've learned

Goals and Deadlines

1. _____ by _____
2. _____ by _____
3. _____ by _____

Cool extras

💬 _____
💬 _____
💬 _____

(Have you worked hard enough today?)   YES   NO

YES   NO   (Are you closer to your goal today?)

Time Spent: ⏱ ⏱ ⏱ ⏱ ⏱

Motivation: 😃 🙂 😐 🙁 😣

/10

Only put off until tomorrow what you are willing to die having left undone
PABLO PICASSO

Today's work

Active Passive

☑ _____ ☐ ☐
☑ _____ ☐ ☐
☑ _____ ☐ ☐
☑ _____ ☐ ☐

Things I have memorized

things I still can't remember

Season

Episode

Minute

⁉ Have you forced yourself today to speak the language with someone?   YES   NO

NOTES

_____
_____
_____

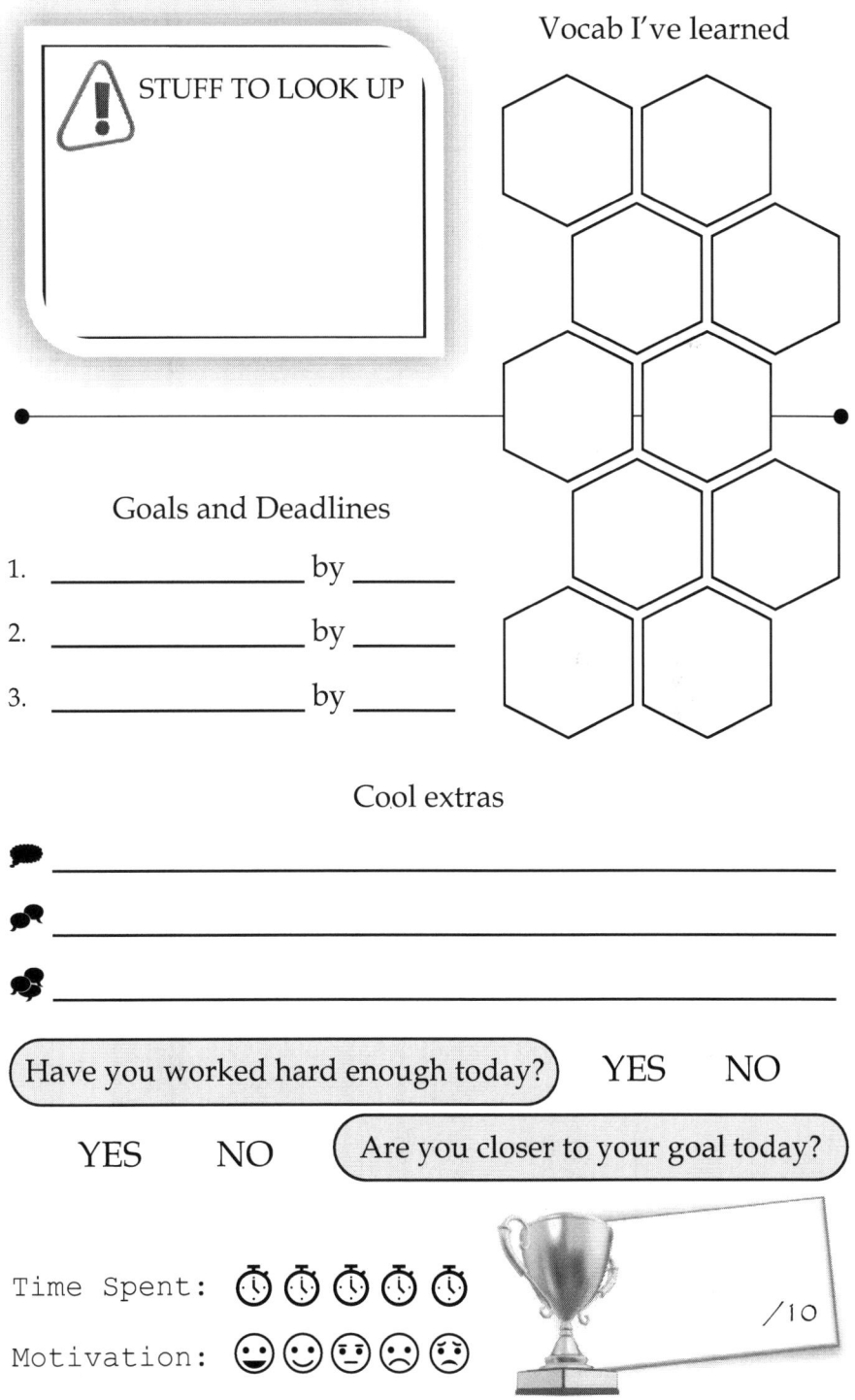

We become what we think about most of the time, and that's the strangest secret
EARL NIGHTINGALE

Today's work

Active Passive

- ☑ _____ ☐ ☐
- ☑ _____ ☐ ☐
- ☑ _____ ☐ ☐
- ☑ _____ ☐ ☐

Things I have memorized

• •
• •
• •

things I still can't remember

Season

Episode

Minute

⁉ Have you forced yourself today to speak the language with someone?   YES   NO

NOTES

_____
_____
_____

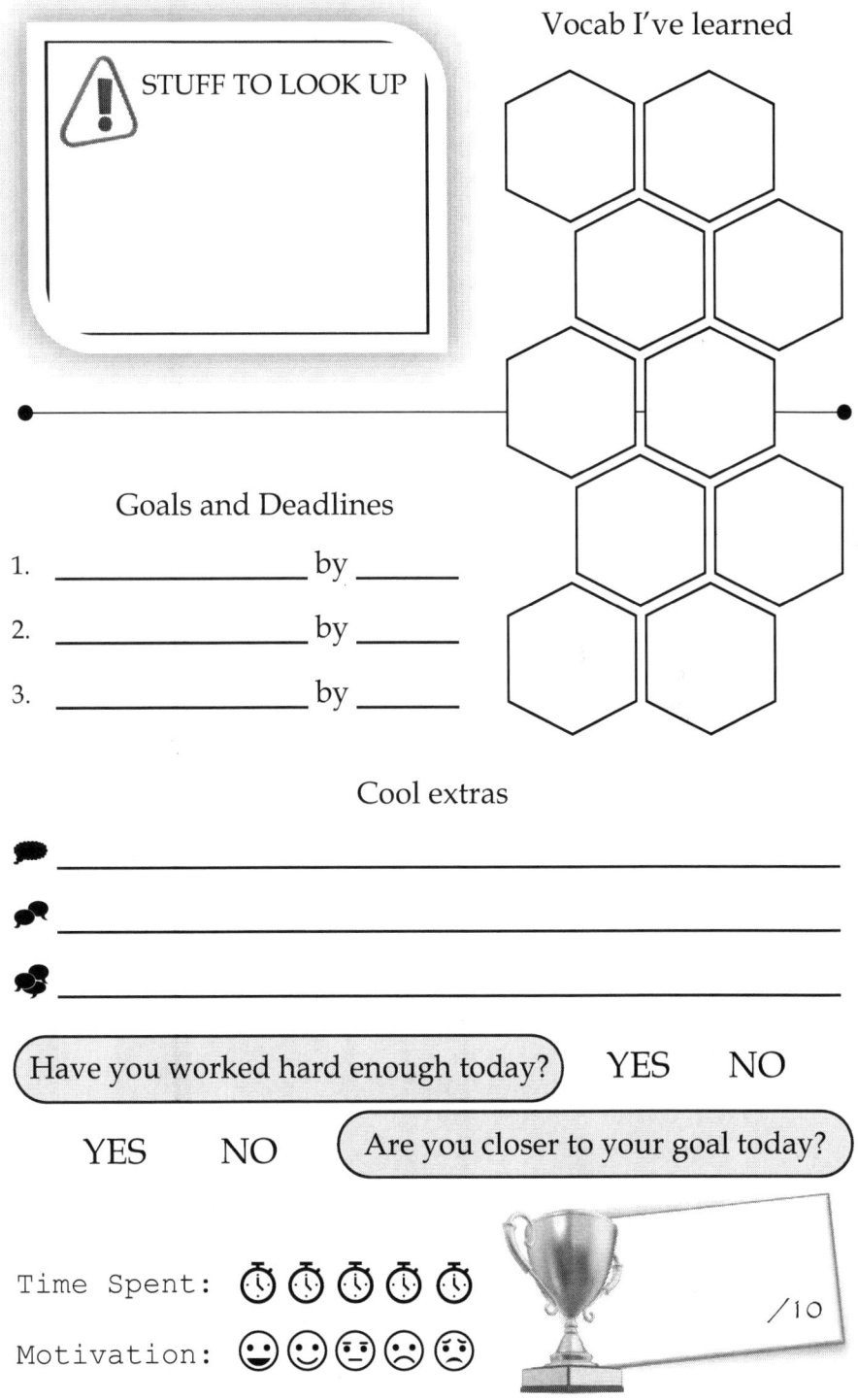

⚠ STUFF TO LOOK UP

Vocab I've learned

Goals and Deadlines

1. _____ by ____
2. _____ by ____
3. _____ by ____

Cool extras

🗨 _____
🗨 _____
🗨 _____

(Have you worked hard enough today?)   YES   NO

YES   NO   (Are you closer to your goal today?)

Time Spent: ⏱ ⏱ ⏱ ⏱ ⏱

Motivation: 😀 🙂 😐 🙁 😟

/10

[180]

The only place where success comes before work is in the dictionary
VIDAL SASSOON

Today's work

Active Passive

☑ _____ ☐ ☐
☑ _____ ☐ ☐
☑ _____ ☐ ☐
☑ _____ ☐ ☐

Things I have memorized

things I still can't remember

Season

Episode

Minute

⁉ Have you forced yourself today to speak the language with someone?   YES   NO

NOTES

_____
_____
_____

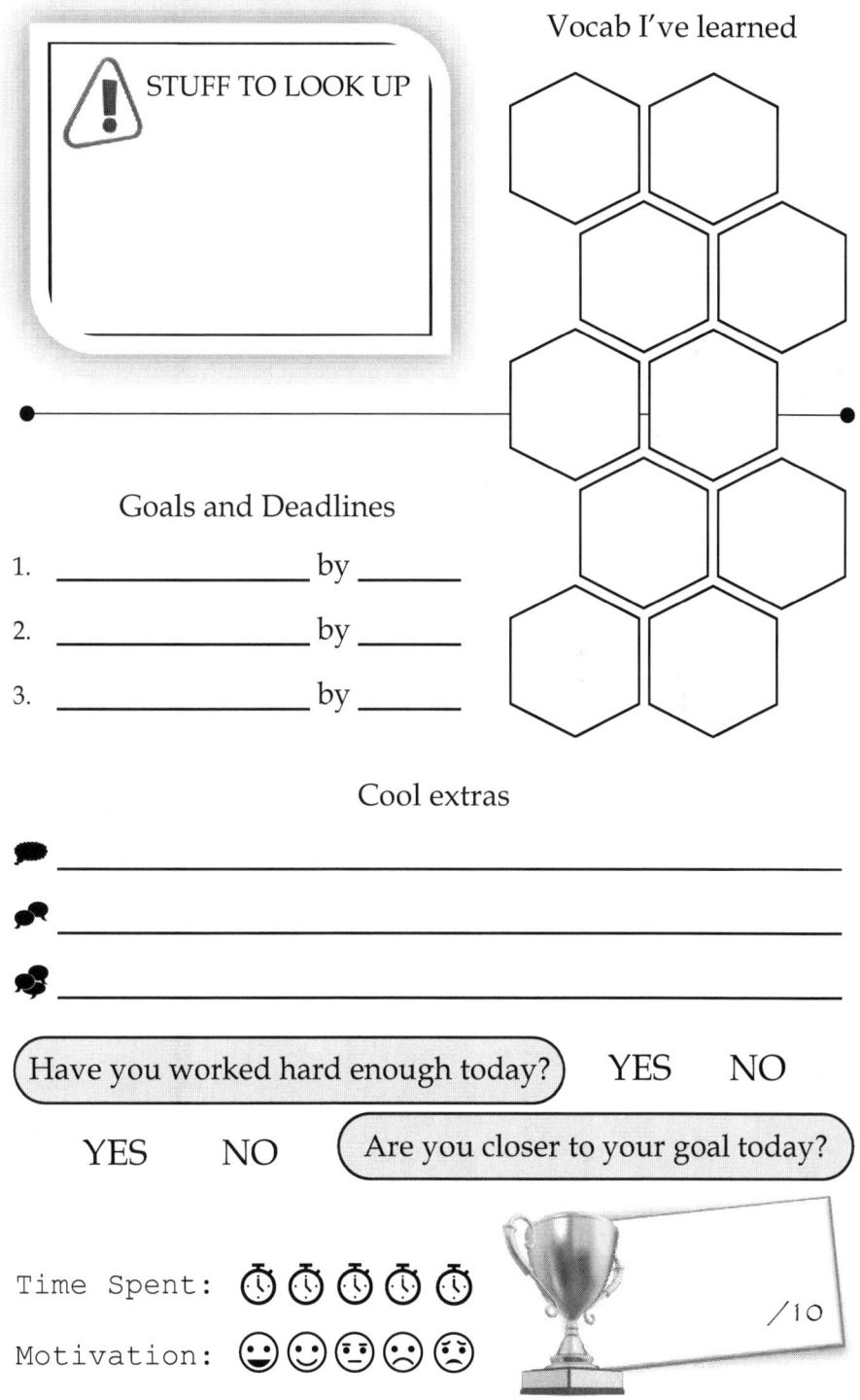

[182]

It's not what you look at that matters, it's what you see
ANONYMOUS

Today's work

Active Passive

☑ _____ ☐ ☐
☑ _____ ☐ ☐
☑ _____ ☐ ☐
☑ _____ ☐ ☐

Things I have memorized

• | •
• | •
• | •

things I still can't remember

Season

Episode

Minute

⁉ Have you forced yourself today to speak the language with someone?   YES   NO

NOTES

_____
_____
_____

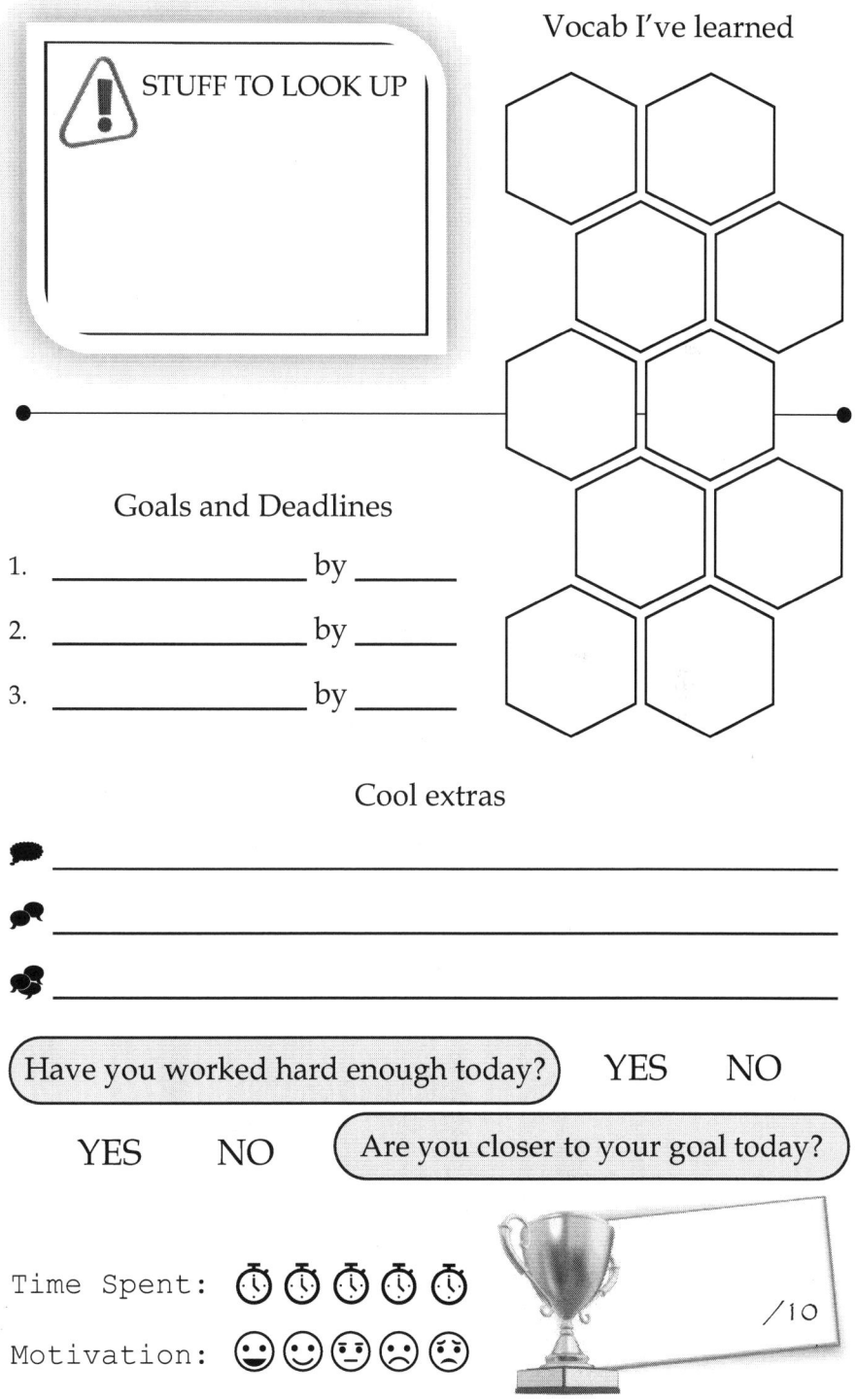

⚠ STUFF TO LOOK UP

Vocab I've learned

Goals and Deadlines

1. _____ by _____
2. _____ by _____
3. _____ by _____

Cool extras

💭 _____
💭 _____
💭 _____

Have you worked hard enough today?   YES   NO

YES   NO   Are you closer to your goal today?

Time Spent: ⏱ ⏱ ⏱ ⏱ ⏱

Motivation: 😀 🙂 😐 🙁 😟

/10

[184]

The road to success and the road to failure are almost exactly the same
COLIN R. DAVIS

Today's work

Active Passive

☑ _____ ☐ ☐
☑ _____ ☐ ☐
☑ _____ ☐ ☐
☑ _____ ☐ ☐

Things I have memorized

•   •
•   •
•   •

things I still can't remember

Season

Episode

Minute

⁉ Have you forced yourself today to speak the language with someone?   YES   NO

NOTES

_____
_____
_____

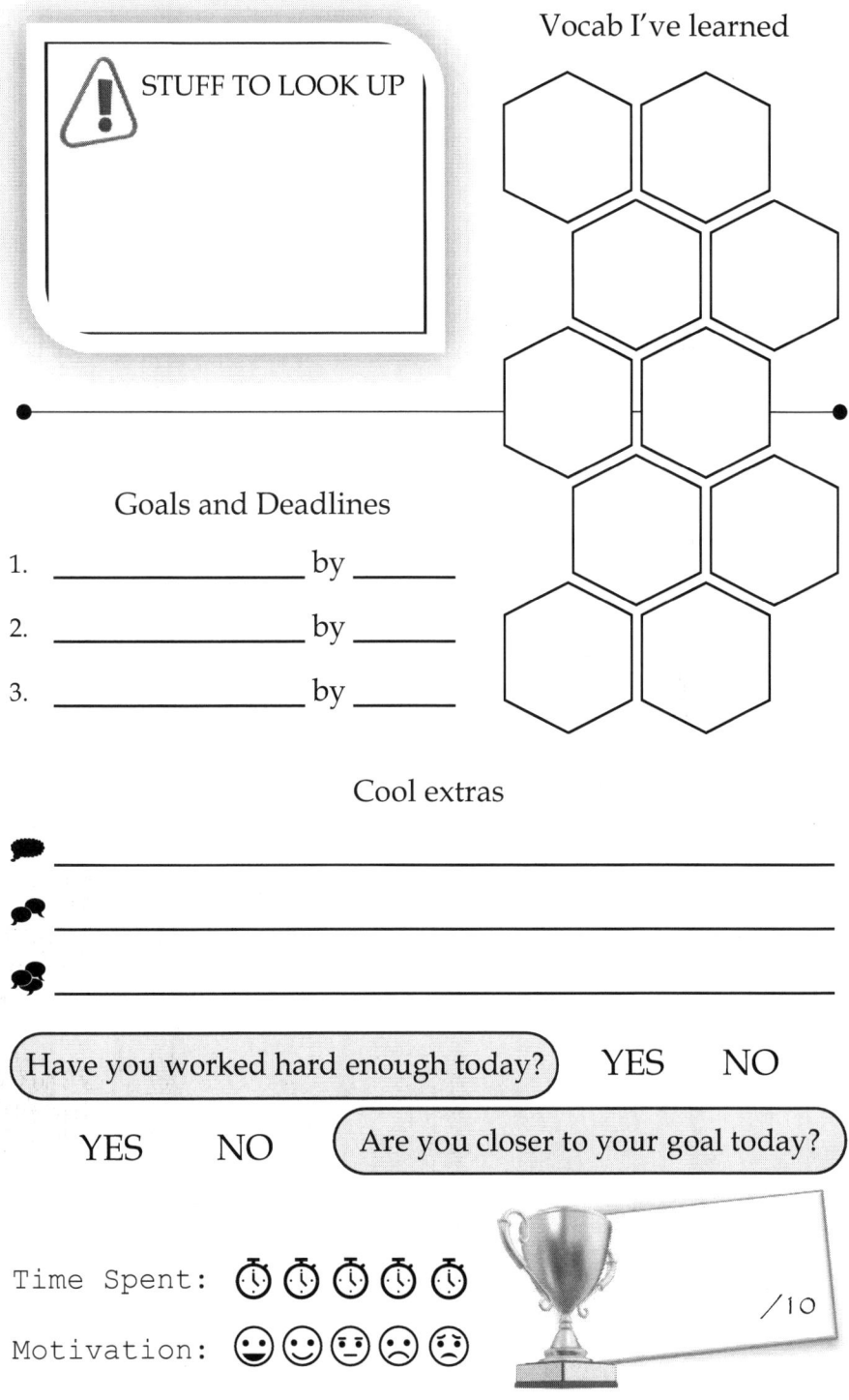

The function of leadership is to produce more leaders, not more followers
RALPH NADER

Today's work

Active Passive

☑ _____ ☐ ☐
☑ _____ ☐ ☐
☑ _____ ☐ ☐
☑ _____ ☐ ☐

Things I have memorized

• | •
• | •
• | •

things I still can't remember

Season

Episode

Minute

⁉ Have you forced yourself today to speak the language with someone?   YES   NO

NOTES

_____
_____
_____

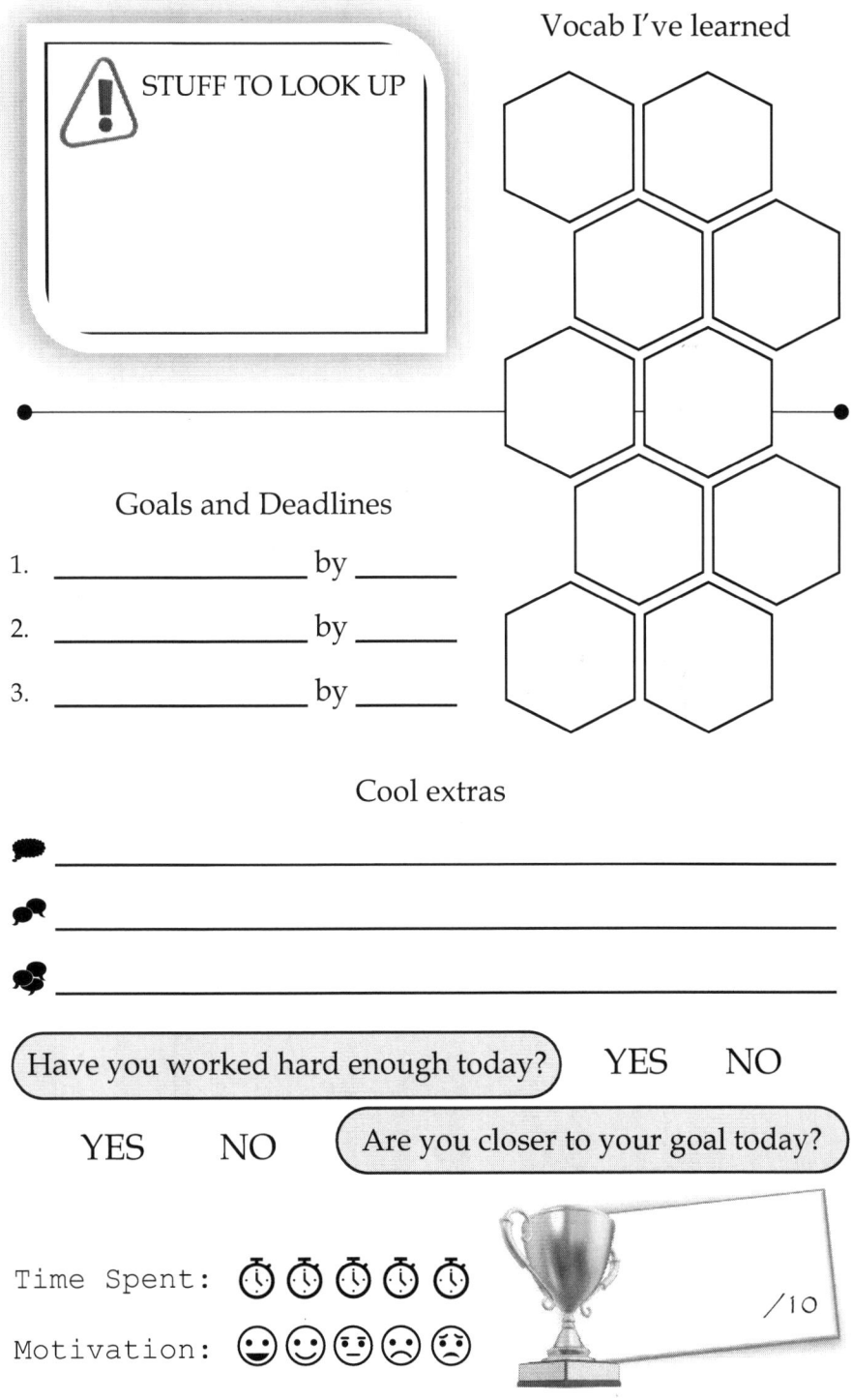

Success is liking yourself, liking what you do, and liking how you do it
MAYA ANGELOU

Today's work

Active Passive

☑ _____ ☐ ☐
☑ _____ ☐ ☐
☑ _____ ☐ ☐
☑ _____ ☐ ☐

Things I have memorized

things I still can't remember

Season

Episode

Minute

⁉ Have you forced yourself today to speak the language with someone?   YES   NO

NOTES

_____
_____
_____

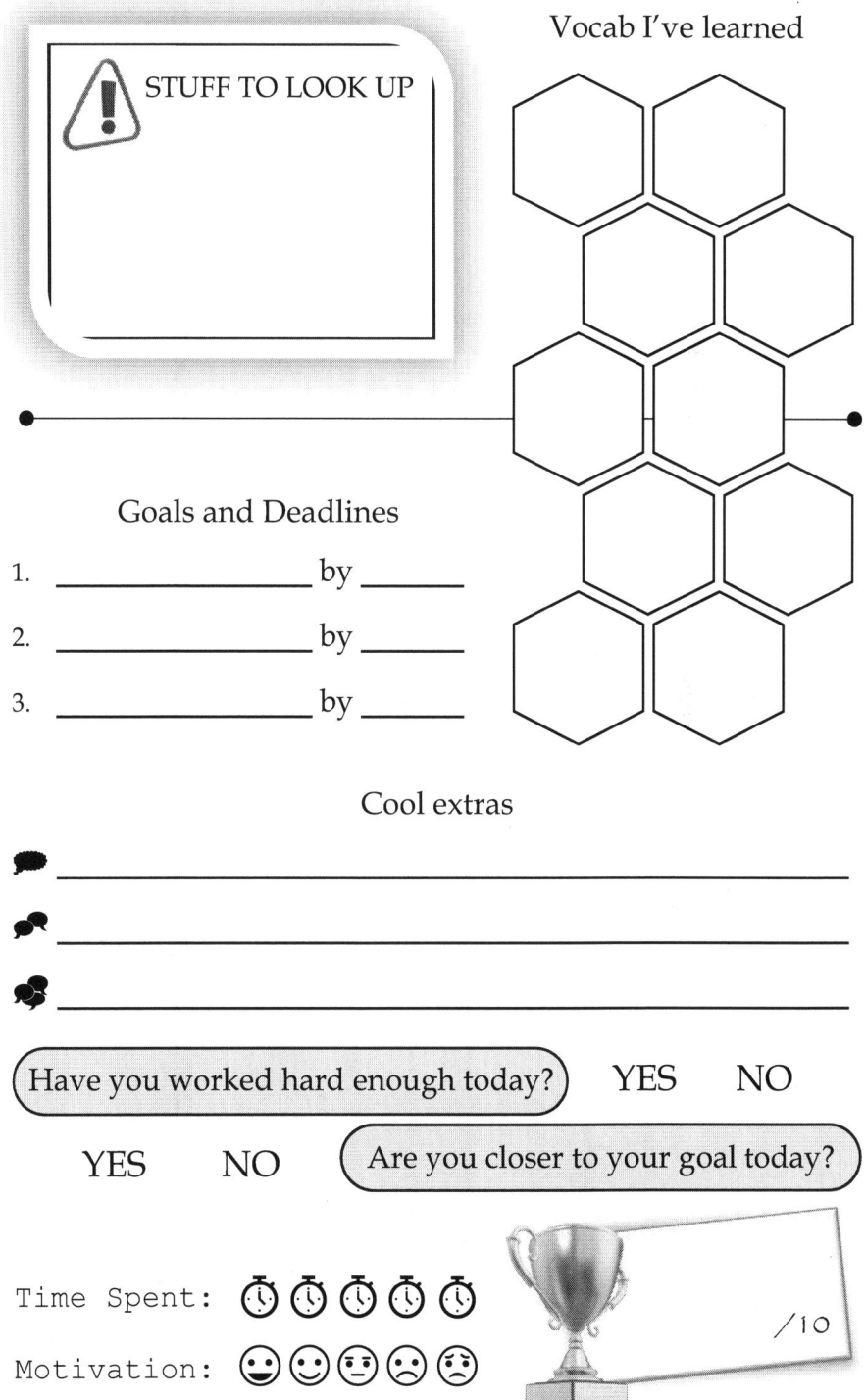

A real entrepreneur is somebody who has no safety net underneath them
HENRY KRAVIS

Today's work

Active Passive

☑ _____ ☐ ☐
☑ _____ ☐ ☐
☑ _____ ☐ ☐
☑ _____ ☐ ☐

Things I have memorized

things I still can't remember

Season

Episode

Minute

⁉ Have you forced yourself today to speak the language with someone?   YES   NO

NOTES

_____
_____
_____

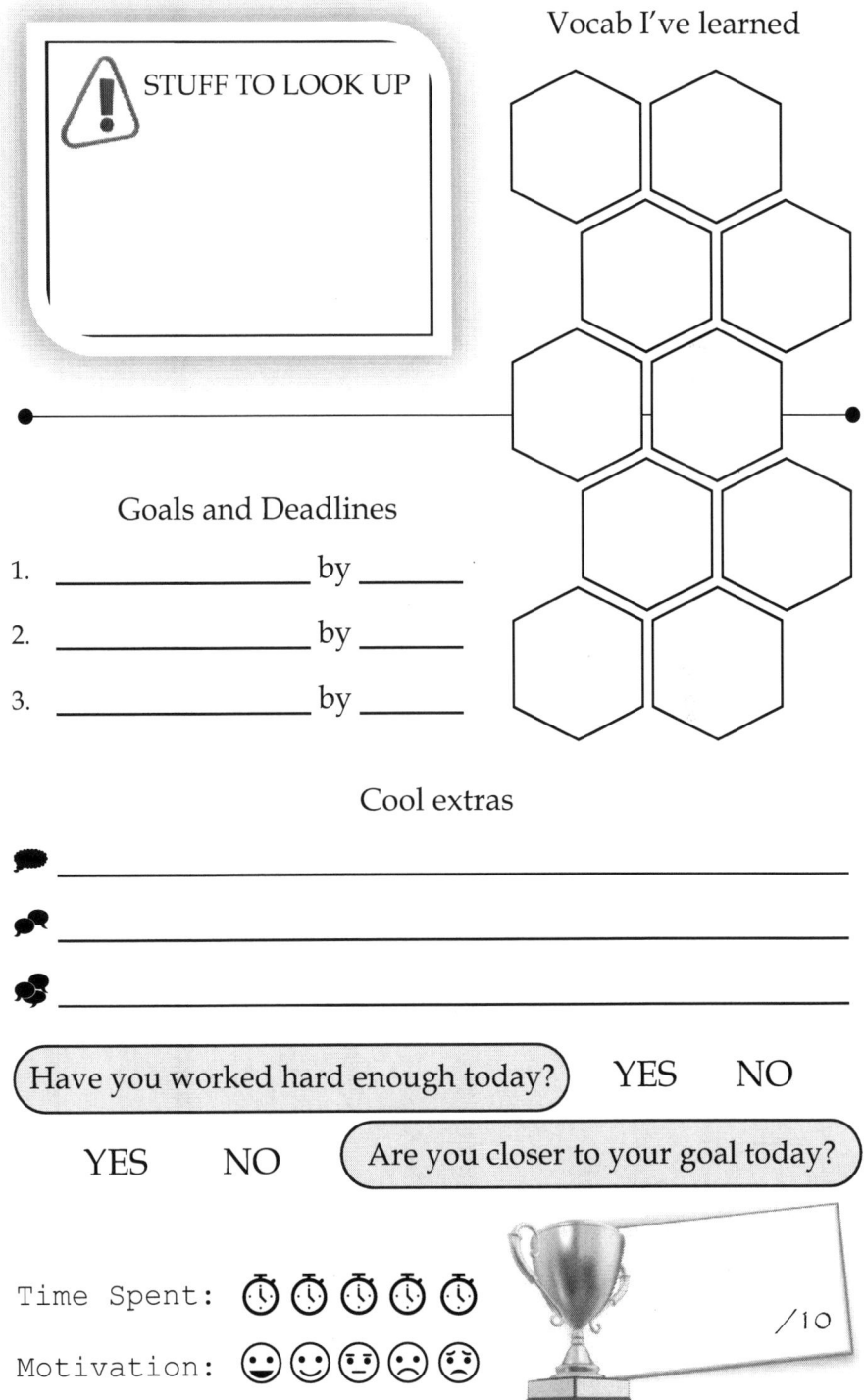

The successful warrior is the average man, with laser-like focus
BRUCE LEE

Today's work

Active Passive

☑ _____ ☐ ☐
☑ _____ ☐ ☐
☑ _____ ☐ ☐
☑ _____ ☐ ☐

Things I have memorized

things I still can't remember

Season

Episode

Minute

⁉ Have you forced yourself today to speak the language with someone?   YES   NO

NOTES

_____
_____
_____

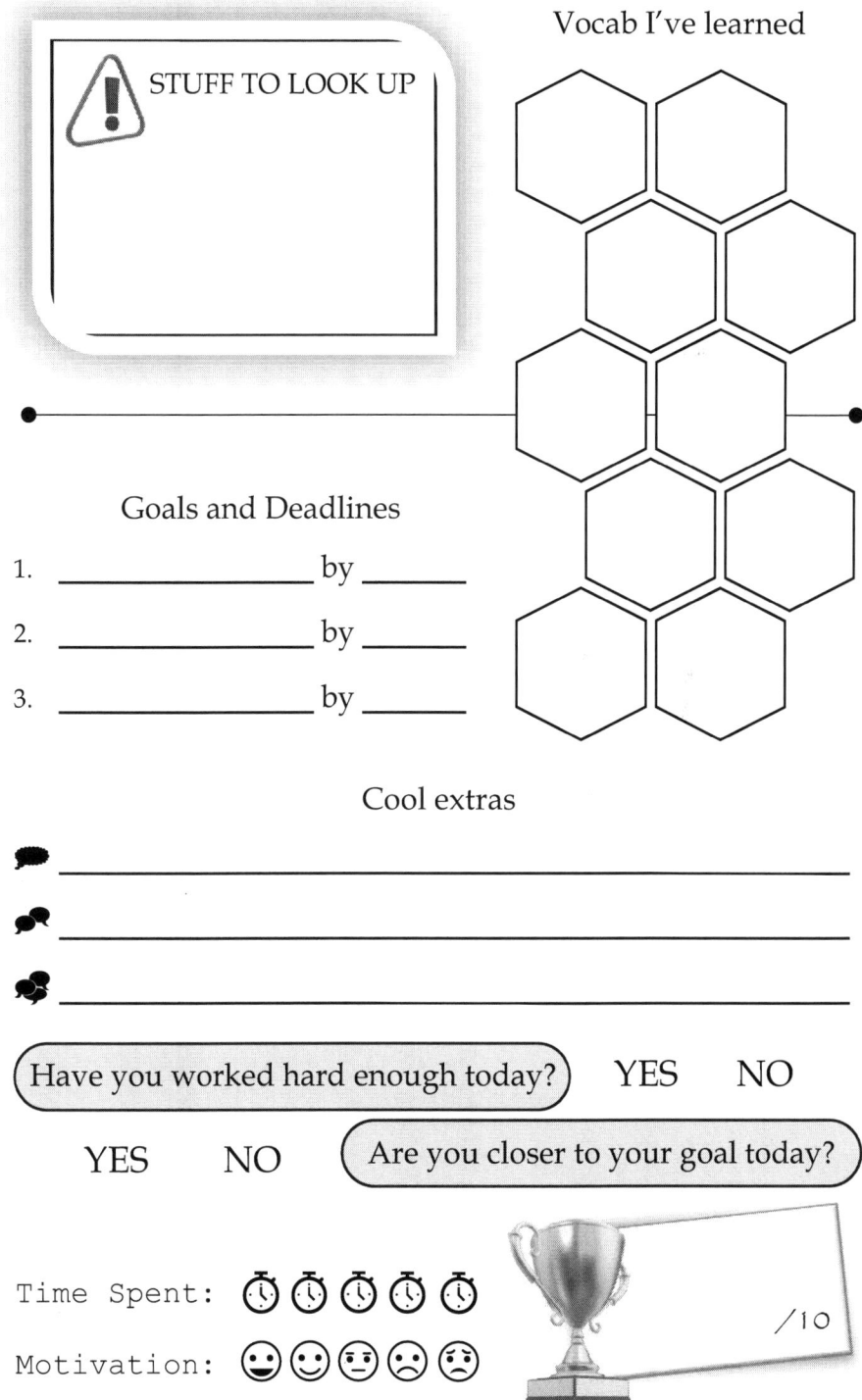

Don't let the fear of losing be greater than the excitement of winning

ROBERT KIYOSAKI

Today's work   Active Passive

☑ _____   ☐ ☐
☑ _____   ☐ ☐
☑ _____   ☐ ☐
☑ _____   ☐ ☐

Things I have memorized

things I still can't remember

Season

Episode

Minute

⁉️ Have you forced yourself today to speak the language with someone?   YES   NO

NOTES

_____
_____
_____

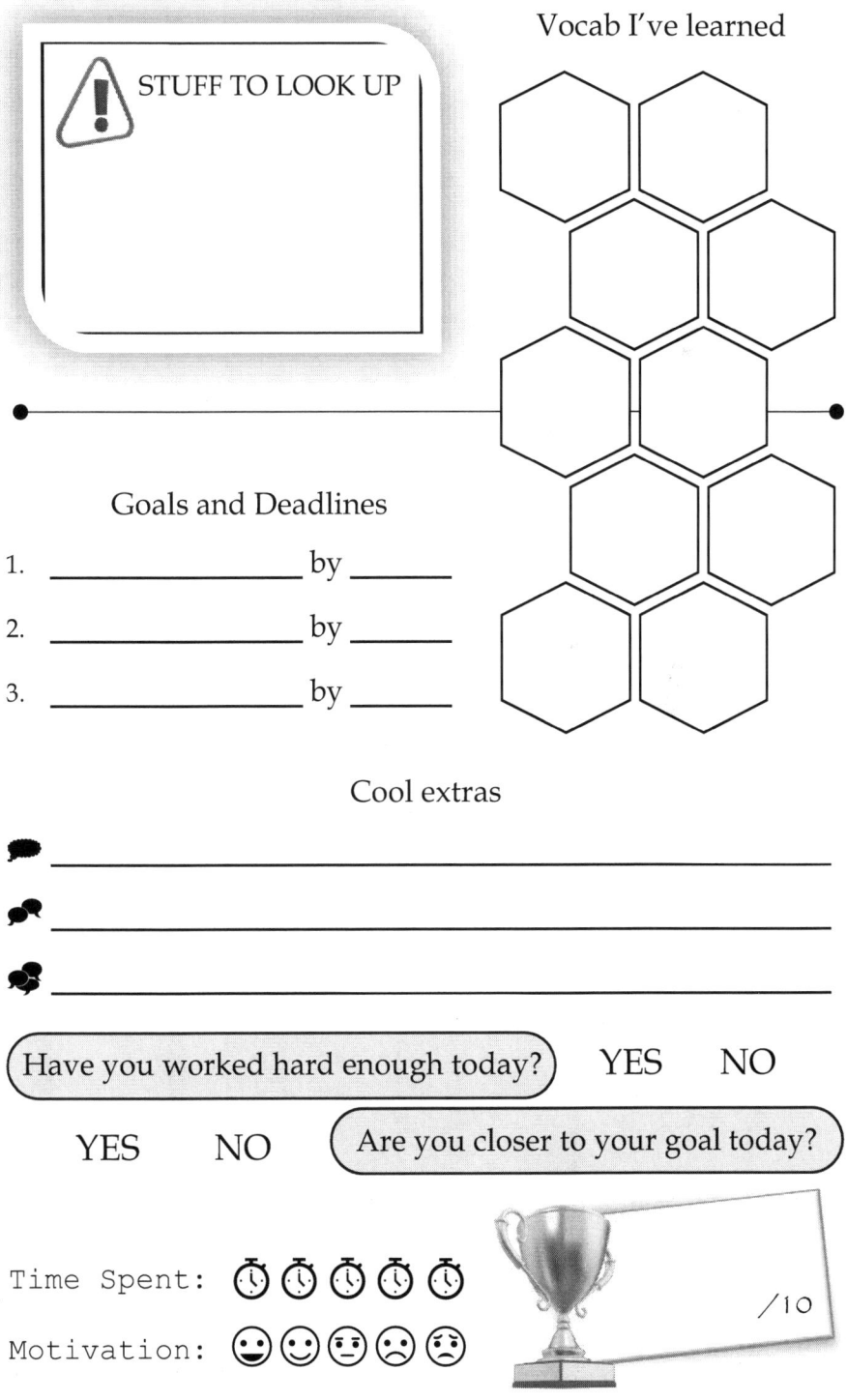

[196]

You must expect great things of yourself before you can do them
MICHAEL JORDAN

Today's work

Active Passive

☑ _____ ☐ ☐
☑ _____ ☐ ☐
☑ _____ ☐ ☐
☑ _____ ☐ ☐

Things I have memorized

things I still can't remember

Season

Episode

Minute

‼ Have you forced yourself today to speak the language with someone?   YES   NO

NOTES

_____
_____
_____

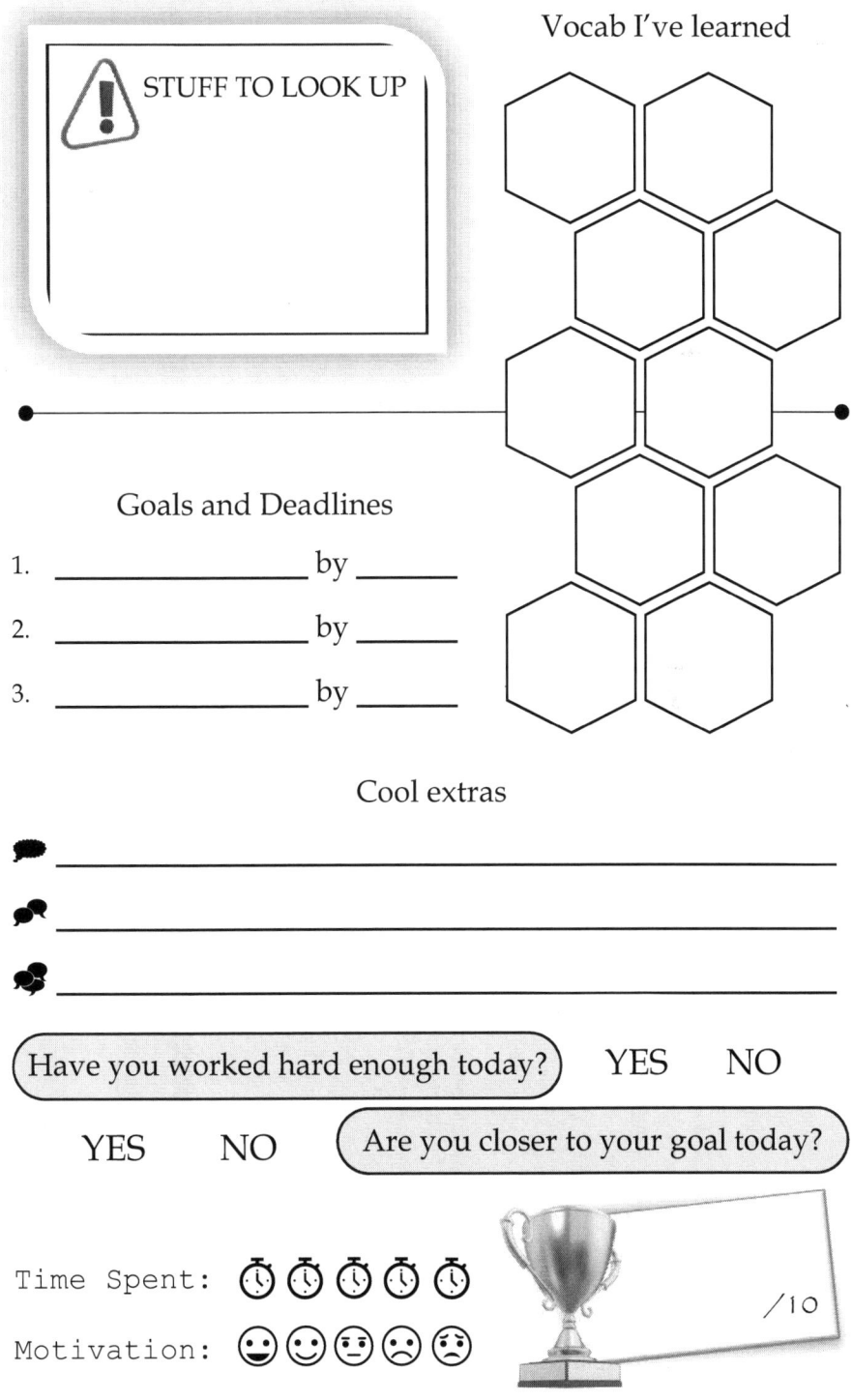

Printed in Poland
by Amazon Fulfillment
Poland Sp. z o.o., Wrocław